MW01077283

COSTA RICA'S
NICOYA PENINSULA

CHRISTOPHER P. BAKER

Contents

COSTA RICA'S
NICOYA PENINSULA

THE NICOYA PENINSULA

Known for its magnificent beaches and a long dry season with sizzling sunshine, the Nicoya Peninsula is a broad, hooked protuberance—130 kilometers long and averaging 50 kilometers wide—separated from the Guanacaste plains by the Río Tempisque and Gulf of Nicoya. Most tourist activity is along the dramatically sculpted Pacific shoreline. Away from the coast, Nicoya is mostly mountainous.

More than three-quarters of Costa Rica's coastal resort infrastructure is in Nicoya, concentrated in northern Nicoya. Several deluxe hotels and a golf course are already in place, with more to follow, tilting the demographics away from eco-conscious travelers toward a more high-end crowd. The opening of the Daniel Oduber International Airport at Liberia in 1996 has significantly boosted arrivals. More

and more mega-resorts are going up. And all along the coast, residential condo complexes have sprouted like palm trees on a wet beach. Aquifers are being drained. Water pollution is rising. And wildlife is disappearing. In all, an ecological disaster is in the making, says alarmed environmentalists, not least thanks to government inaction in the face of developers who simply don't care. Finally, in April 2008, President Oscar Arias issued a temporary decree imposing new restrictions on coastal construction, and MINAE (the governmental environmental body) actually began tearing down offending buildings.

Though each beach community has its own distinct appeal, most remain barefoot and button-down, appealing to laid-back travelers who can hang with the locals and appreciate the

© CHRISTOPHER P. BAKER

HIGHLIGHTS

(Guaitíl: Ancient pottery traditions are kept alive at this charming village, where you can witness ceramics being crafted in age-old fashion (page 18).

(Tempisque Safari Ecological Adventure: Remote it may be, but this wildlife rescue center and zoo is one of the nation's finest. A visit includes a wildlife-filled boat tour on the Río Tempisque (page 19).

(Marino Las Baulas National Park: Here, surfers can enjoy consistent action while nature lovers can kayak or take boat trips in search of crocodiles, birds, and other wildlife in the reserve behind the beach. The highlight in season is a chance to witness giant leatherback turtles laying eggs (page 38).

(Ostional National Wildlife Refuge: Site of a unique mass turtle nesting, this remote reserve has few services, but the expe-rience of witnessing an *arribada* will sear your memory for the rest of your life (page 57).

(Nosara: Beautiful beaches, cracking surf, plentiful wildlife, and a broad choice of accom-modations combine to make Nosara a choice destination (page 60).

(Isla Tortuga: Stunning beaches, nature trails, warm turquoise waters, and plenty of water sports await passengers on day cruises to this gorgeous little isle off southeast Nicoya (page 82).

(Cabo Blanco Absolute Wildlife Reserve: This remote reserve is unrivaled locally for wildlife viewing, with all the main critters on show (page 89).

(Santa Teresa and Malpaís: These burgeoning yet offbeat communities are the gateway to Playa Santa Teresa, the perfect spot to bag some rays, ride the waves, and chill (page 90).

LOOK FOR **(** TO FIND RECOMMENDED SIGHTS, ACTIVITIES, DINING, AND LODGING.

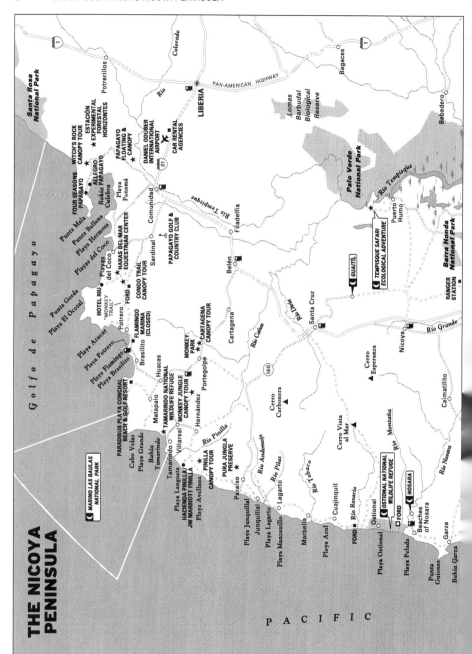

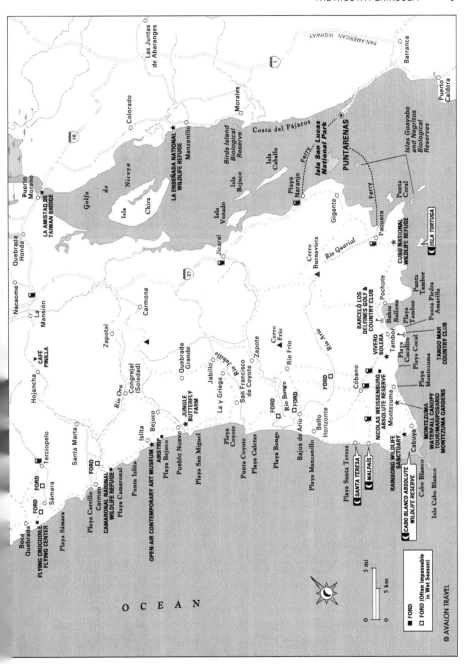

© AVALON TRAVEL

wildlife that comes down to the shore. This is particularly so of the southern beaches. Waves pump ashore along much of the coastline, and many beaches have been discovered by surfers, who are opening up heretofore hidden sections of jungle-lined shore. Newly cut roads are linking the last pockets of the erstwhile inaccessible Pacific coast, though negotiating the dirt highways is always tricky—and part of the fun.

Predominantly dry to the north and progressively moist to the south, the peninsula offers a variety of ecosystems, with no shortage of opportunities for nature-viewing; monkeys, coatis, sloths, and other wildlife species inhabit the forests along the shore. Two of the premier nesting sites for marine turtles are here. The offshore waters are beloved of scuba divers and for sportfishing. And water sports are well developed.

The best time to visit is December–April, when rain is virtually unheard of (average annual rainfall is less than 150 centimeters in some areas). The rainy season generally arrives in May and lasts until November, turning dirt roads into muddy (and often impassable) quagmires sure to test your driving skills to the max. September and October are the wettest months. The so-called Papagayo winds—heavy northerlies *(nortes)*—blow strongly from January (sometimes earlier) through March and are felt mostly in northern Nicoya. Surfers rave about the rainy season (May–Nov.), when swells are consistent and waves—fast and tubular—can be 1.5 meters or more.

The downside—besides the immense overdevelopment of condominium projects—is the skyrocketing crime in Nicoya. In 2006 the police chief called it an emergency.

PLANNING YOUR TIME

Nicoya's beaches require a month to sample in earnest. One week to 10 days should be sufficient to sample two or three of the best beaches. In the north, Tamarindo makes a good base for exploring farther afield, but the poor state of coast roads is not conducive to round-trip travel. It's perhaps best to keep moving on, north or south.

If white-sand floats your boat, head to **Playa Flamingo** or nearby **Playa Conchal,** which is backed by the country's largest resort hotel, complete with golf course and water sports. **Montezuma,** a charming little community on the southern tip of Nicoya, also has a superb white-sand beach.

There's no shortage of options for accommodations for any budget, although reservations are highly recommended for holiday periods, when Ticos flock. The most complete services and range of accommodations are found at **Tamarindo,** a surfing center with a wide range of other activities, plus several fine restaurants. **Playas del Coco** and adjacent beach resorts of Ocotal and Hermosa, while less attractive than other beaches, are bases for sportfishing and scuba diving. Surfers can choose from dozens of beaches: the best begin at Playa Grande and extend south to **Malpaís** and **Playa Santa Teresa;** many are remote and have few, if any, facilities. **Playa Camaronal to Manzanillo,** with several superb and lonesome beaches—almost all favored by marine turtles for nesting—is a fabulous adventure by four-wheel drive.

Two nature experiences stand out: a visit to **Marino Las Baulas National Park** to see the leatherback turtles laying eggs, and the **Ostional National Wildlife Refuge** during its unique mass invasions of olive ridley turtles. These are, for me, the most momentous guaranteed wildlife encounters in Costa Rica. **Curú National Wildlife Refuge** and **Cabo Blanco Wildlife Refuge** offer their own nature highlights, as does **Nosara,** another prime surf destination.

Don't leave Nicoya without calling in at the village of **Guaitíl,** where Chorotega families make pottery in the same fashion their ancestors did one thousand years ago. Nearby, **Barra Honda National Park** is the nation's preeminent spelunking site.

Getting to the Coast

Driving from San José to the coast resorts takes a minimum of four or five hours. A single highway (Hwy. 21) runs north–south along the eastern plains of Nicoya, linking Liberia with the towns

FERRIES TO AND FROM NICOYA

Two car-and-passenger ferries and a passengers-only ferry cross the Río Tempisque and Gulf of Nicoya, shortening the driving distance to or from the Nicoya Peninsula. In high season and on weekends, lines can get long, and you should get there at least an hour before departure times, which change frequently. Check ahead!

PUNTARENAS TO PAQUERA

Ferry Naviera Tambor (tel. 506/2661-2084, ferrypeninsular@racsa.co.cr) ferries departs Avenida 3, Calles 33, in Puntarenas for Paquera daily every two or three hours 5 A.M.-9 P.M. Return ferries depart Paquera 5 A.M.-7 P.M. ($2 pedestrians, $9 car and passengers). Take this ferry to reach Montezuma and Malpaís.

A passengers-only *lancha* (water-taxi, tel. 506/2661-0515) departs Puntarenas for Paquera at 11:30 A.M. and 4 P.M. from Avenida 3, Calles 2/Central. Return ferries depart Paquera at 7:30 A.M. and 2 P.M. ($1.25 adults, $1 for bicycles and children).

Buses (tel. 506/642-0219) meet the ferries and depart Paquera for Cóbano at 6:15 A.M., 8:30 A.M., 10:30 A.M., noon, 2:30 P.M., 4:30 P.M., and 6:30 P.M.; and from Cóbano to Paquera at 3:45 A.M., 5:45 A.M., 8:30 A.M., 10:30 A.M., 12:15 P.M., 2:30 P.M., and 6:30 P.M.

PUNTARENAS TO NARANJO

Playa Naranjo is two-thirds of the way down the Nicoya Peninsula and makes a perfect landing stage if you're heading to Sámara or Nosara.

The **Coonatramar Ferry** (tel. 506/2661-1069, www.coonatramar.com) departs Puntarenas from Avenida 3, Calles 33/35, at 6:30 A.M., 10 A.M., 2:30 P.M., and 7:30 P.M. ($1.60 adult, $0.75 child, $3 motorcycle, $10.50 car). The return ferry departs Playa Naranjo at 8 A.M., 12:30 P.M., 5:30 P.M., and 9 P.M. Buy your ticket from a booth to the left of the gates at Naranjo, but be sure to park in line first.

Buses meet the ferry for Jicaral, Coyote, Bejuco, Carmona, and Nicoya.

---

of Filadelfia, Santa Cruz, and Nicoya, then south (deteriorating all the while) to Playa Naranjo, Paquera, Tambor, and Montezuma. Spur roads snake west over the mountains, connecting beach communities to civilization. Excepting a short section south of Sámara, no paved highway links the various beach resorts, which are connected by a network of dirt roads roughly paralleling the coast; at times you will need to head inland to connect with another access road. Plan accordingly, and allow much more time than may be obvious by looking at a map. Several sections require river fordings—no easy task in wet season, when many rivers are impassable (the section between Sámara and Malpaís is the most daunting and adventurous of wet season drives in the country). A four-wheel-drive vehicle is essential. It's wise to fill up wherever you find gas available (often it will be poured from a

can—and cost about double what it would at a true gas station). The roads are blanketed with choking dust in dry season, although every year sees more and more roads paved.

The Pan-American Highway (Hwy. 1) via Liberia gives relatively easy access to the northern Nicoya via Highway 21, which runs west for 20 kilometers to Comunidad, gateway to Bahía de Culebra, the Playas de Coco region, and Tamarindo.

The main access to central Nicoya from Highway 1 is via the Puente de Amistad con Taiwan (Friendship with Taiwan Bridge), about 27 kilometers west of Highway 1 (the turnoff is 2 kilometers north of Limonal). Highway 18 connects with Highway 21.

Daily car and passenger ferries also cross from Puntarenas to Naranjo (for central beaches) and Paquera (for Montezuma and Malpaís).

Highway 2 to Santa Cruz

The Río Tempisque is spanned by the **Puente de Amistad con Taiwan,** a suspension bridge whose construction was a gift from the Taiwanese government. On its west bank, Highway 18 continues 15 kilometers to a T-junction with Highway 21 at **Puerto Viejo;** the town of Nicoya, the regional capital, is 15 kilometers north of the junction (Highway 21 loops north via Santa Cruz and Filadelfia to reconnect with Highway 1 at Liberia).

Tempisque Eco-Adventures & Canopy Tour (tel. 506/2687-1212, ecoadventures@ racsa.co.cr), four kilometers west of the bridge, has a canopy tour ($40) and offers boat trips to Palo Verde National Park at 9:30 A.M. and 1 P.M. ($45).

BARRA HONDA NATIONAL PARK

The 2,295-hectare Parque Nacional Barra Honda (tel. 506/2659-1551 or 2659-1099, 8 A.M.–4 P.M., $10 admission), 13 kilometers west of the Río Tempisque, is a rugged upland area known for its limestone caverns dating back 70 million years (42 caverns have been discovered to date). Skeletons, utensils, and ornaments dating back to 300 B.C. have been discovered inside the Nicoya Cave. The deepest cavern thus far explored is the 240-meter-deep Santa Ana Cave, known for its Hall of Pearls, full of stalactites and stalagmites.

The only caverns open to the public are **Terciopelo Cave** (children must be 12 or over), with three chambers reached via an exciting 30-meter vertical ladder, then a sloping plane that leads to the bottom, 63 meters down; and **La Cuevita.** Within, Mushroom Hall is named for the shape of its calcareous formations; the Hall of the Caverns has large Medusa-like formations, including a figure resembling a lion's head. And columns in "The Organ" produce musical tones when struck.

Some of the caverns are frequented by bats, including the Pozo Hediondo (Fetid Pit) Cave, which is named for the quantity of excrement accumulated by its abundant bat population. Blind salamanders and endemic fish species have also evolved in the caves. Caverna Nicoya contains pre-Columbian petroglyphs.

Above ground, the hilly dry forest terrain is a refuge for howler monkeys, deer, agoutis, peccaries, kinkajous, anteaters, and many bird species, including scarlet macaws. The park tops out at Mount Barra Honda (442 m), which has intriguing rock formations and provides an excellent view of the Gulf of Nicoya. Las Cascadas are strange limestone formations formed by calcareous sedimentation along a riverbed.

Guides and Tours

Cave descents are allowed 7:30 A.M.–1 P.M. daily May–November, and until 2 P.M. December–April, except Holy Week ($36 s, $52 d four hours, including entrance, guide, and cave equipment; the price varies depending on number of participants). For cave descents, you must be accompanied by a guide from the **Asociación de Guías Ecologistas de Barra Honda,** which also has guided walks ($10 pp) plus nighttime tours ($7 pp, three person minimum) in dry season. Budget at least four hours to visit the caves. You can drive to about 1.5 kilometers beyond the park entrance, after which you're on foot: it's hot, steep, and there are mosquitoes.

Reservations are required for the Sendero Las Cascadas, which leads to waterfalls; guided tours only.

Accommodations

There's a campsite ($2 pp) at the ranger station, which also has simple cabins for volunteers willing to help with trail maintenance and other projects. It has basic showers and toilets plus picnic tables and water. At last visit, meal service was being planned.

One kilometer before the park entrance, **Hotel Barra Honda** (tel. 506/2659-1003, $15 s/d) is set in spacious tree-shaded grounds and has a simple open-air restaurant. It offers horseback rides. The 10 basic modern cabins have

Parroquia San Blas church

fans and spacious modern bathrooms. Of similar standard, **Las Cavernas Tourist Lodge** (tel. 506/2659-1574, fax 506/2659-1573, $12 pp), 400 meters from the park entrance, has five bare-bones rooms with cold-water private bathrooms and a delightful cowboy-style restaurant and bar decorated with yokes and saddles. It has a small pool.

Getting There

The turnoff for the Nacaome (Barra Honda) ranger station is 1.5 kilometers east of Puerto Viejo and 15 kilometers west of the Tempisque Bridge. From here, an all-weather gravel road leads via Nacaome, all the while deteriorating (4WD recommended); signs point the way to the entrance, about six kilometers farther via Santa Ana.

A Tracopa-Alfaro (tel. 506/2222-2666) bus from San José to Nicoya will drop you at the turnoff for the park; Las Cavernas will send a pickup by prior arrangement. A bus departs Nicoya for Santa Ana and Nacaome at 12:30 P.M. daily, plus 4 P.M. on Monday, Wednesday, and Friday; you can walk to the park entrance. You

can also enter the park from the east via a dirt road (from Quebrada Honda, off Highway 21 immediately east of Nicoya township.

NICOYA

Nicoya, about 78 kilometers south of Liberia, is Costa Rica's oldest colonial city. Today it bustles as the agricultural and administrative heart of the region. The town is named for the Chorotega chief who presented Spanish conquistador Gil González Dávila with gold. The native heritage is still apparent.

The only sight of interest is the **Parroquia San Blas** (tel. 506/2685-5109, 8 A.M.–4 P.M. Mon.–Fri., 8 A.M.–noon Sat.) church built in the 16th century, gleaming anew following a restoration and decorating the town's peaceful plaza. It contains a few pre-Columbian icons and religious antiques.

Accommodations

The **Hotel Venecia** (tel. 506/2685-5325, $15 pp with fan, $20 with a/c), on the north side of the plaza, has 37 clean but basic rooms. Newer, nicer units in a two-story unit are to the rear.

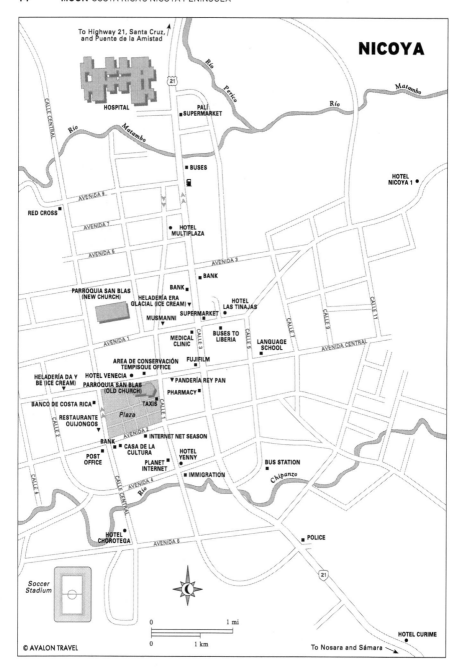

NICOYA

To Highway 21, Santa Cruz, and Puente de la Amistad

CALLE CENTRAL

Río Matambo

Río Perico

Río

Matambo

HOSPITAL

PALÍ SUPERMARKET

BUSES

HOTEL NICOYA 1

RED CROSS

AVENIDA 9

AVENIDA 7

HOTEL MULTIPLAZA

AVENIDA 5

AVENIDA 3

BANK

PARROQUIA SAN BLAS (NEW CHURCH)

BANK

HELADERÍA ERA GLACIAL (ICE CREAM)

HOTEL LAS TINAJAS

MUSMANNI

SUPERMARKET

CALLE 11

CALLE 9

CALLE 7

MEDICAL CLINIC

BUSES TO LIBERIA

LANGUAGE SCHOOL

CALLE 5

CALLE 3

AVENIDA 1

AVENIDA CENTRAL

AREA DE CONSERVACIÓN TEMPISQUE OFFICE

FUJIFILM

HELADERÍA DA Y BE (ICE CREAM)

HOTEL VENECIA

PARROQUIA SAN BLAS (OLD CHURCH)

PANDERÍA REY PAN

PHARMACY

BANCO DE COSTA RICA

TAXIS

CALLE 1

Plaza

CALLE 2

RESTAURANTE OUIJONGOS

AVENIDA 2

INTERNET NET SEASON

BANK

CASA DE LA CULTURA

POST OFFICE

PLANET INTERNET

HOTEL YENNY

BUS STATION

Chipanzo

IMMIGRATION

CALLE 4

AVENIDA 4

CALLE CENTRAL

Río

HOTEL CHOROTEGA

AVENIDA 6

POLICE

Soccer Stadium

0   1 mi

0   1 km

© AVALON TRAVEL

To Nosara and Sámara

HOTEL CURIME

FESTIVAL OF LA VIRGEN DE GUADALUPE

Try to visit Nicoya on December 12, when villagers carry a dark-skinned image of La Virgen de Guadalupe through the streets accompanied by flutes, drums, and dancers. The festival combines the Catholic celebration of the Virgin of Guadalupe with the traditions of the Chorotega legend of La Yequita (Little Mare), a mare that interceded to prevent twin brothers from fighting to the death for the love of a princess. The religious ceremony is a good excuse for bullfights, explosive fireworks (*bombas*), concerts, and general merriment. Many locals get sozzled on *chicha*, a heady brew made from fermented corn and sugar and drunk from hollow gourds.

It has secure parking. Budget options of similar standard include **Hotel Chorotega** (Calle Central, Avenida 6, tel. 506/2685-5245, $7 pp shared bath, $8 s or $12 d private bath, $14 s or $18 d with hot water and TV); and the similarly priced **Hotel Yenny** (Calle 1, Avenida 4, tel. 506/2685-5050); and **Hotel Las Tinajas** (Avenida 1, Calle 5, tel./fax 506/2685-5081).

The best bargain is **Hotel Multiplaza** (tel. 506/2685-3535, Calle 1, Avenidas 5/7, $15 pp), which has 25 dark but spacious air-conditioned rooms with fans, comfy mattresses, and cable TV, but cold water only. There's a small café outside. Slightly more upscale, the **Hotel Nicoya I** (tel. 506/2686-6331, $25 s, $30 d) has eight air-conditioned rooms with fan and private bathrooms with hot water.

The nicest place is **Hotel Río Tempisque de Lujo** (tel. 506/2686-6650, $40 s, $45 d), on Highway 21, 800 meters north of the junction for Nicoya township, with 30 well-lit, spacious, air-conditioned cabins in groomed gardens set back from the road for peace and quiet. Each has two double beds, cable TV, refrigerator, coffeemaker, microwave, and pleasing bathrooms with hair dryer and hot water.

There's a swimming pool and whirlpool tub in lush gardens.

Food

The best bet in town is **Restaurante Ouijongos** (tel. 506/2686-4748, 11 A.M.–10 P.M. daily) on the west side of the plaza. It serves excellent seafood, including ceviche ($5) and shrimp in oyster sauce ($12), plus meat dishes and *casados* (set lunches, $3).

There's a **Musmanni** bakery at Calle 1, Avenida 1. **Heladería Da y Be,** on the northwest side of the plaza, sells ice cream, as does **Heladería Era Glacial** (Calle 3, Avenida 1), a delightful coffee shop opposite **Super Compro** supermarket.

Information and Services

MINAE (tel. 506/2686-6760, fax 506/2685-5667, 8 A.M.–4 P.M. Mon.–Fri.), on the north side of the plaza, administers the Tempisque Conservation Area. It is not set up to serve tourists.

The **hospital** (tel. 506/2685-5066) is on the north side of town, and there are several medical clinics. The **post office** (Avenida 2, Calle Central) is open 7:30 A.M.–5:30 P.M. daily. The **police station** (tel. 506/2685-5559) is 500 meters south of the town center, on Calle 3, which has four banks. You can make international calls from **Planet Internet** (Avenida 4, Calle 1, tel. 506/2685-4281, 8 A.M.–8 P.M. Mon.–Sat.) or **Internet Net Season** (Avenida 2, Calles Central/1, tel. 506/2685-4045).

Inmigración (Avenida 4, Calle 1, tel. 506/2686-4155, 8 A.M.–4 P.M. Mon.–Fri.) can issue visa extensions.

Instituto Guanacasteco de Idiomas (tel. 506/2686-6948, www.spanishcostarica.com) offers Spanish-language instruction.

Getting There

Tracopa Alfaro buses (tel. 506/2222-2666) depart San José for Nicoya from Calle 14, Avenidas 3/5, at 5:30 A.M., 7:30 A.M., 10 A.M., noon, 1 P.M., 3 P.M., 5 P.M., and 6:30 P.M. daily ($5, six hours). Buses also serve Nicoya from Liberia every 30 minutes, 4:30 A.M.–8:20 P.M. daily; and from Santa Cruz hourly, 6 A.M.–9 P.M. daily.

Buses (tel. 506/2685-5032) depart Nicoya for San José from Avenida 4, Calle 3, at 3 A.M., 4:30 A.M., 5:15 A.M., 9:15 A.M., noon, 2:45 P.M., and 5 P.M. daily; for Playa Naranjo at 5:15 A.M. and 1 P.M. daily; for Sámara 13 times daily 5 A.M.–9:45 P.M.; and for Nosara at 5 A.M., 10 A.M., noon, and 3 P.M. daily. Buses also serve other towns throughout the peninsula.

SANTA CRUZ

This small town, 20 kilometers north of Nicoya, is the "National Folklore City" and a gateway to Playas Tamarindo and Junquillal, 30 kilometers to the west. Santa Cruz is renowned for its traditional music, food, and dance, which can be sampled during *fiestas cívicas* each January 15 and July 25.

The ruin of an old church (toppled by an earthquake in 1950) stands next to its modern replacement with a star-shaped roof and beautiful stained glass. The leafy plaza—**Parque Central**—boasts a Mayan-style cupola, lampshades with Mayan motifs, and monuments on each corner, including a "bucking bronco" (cowboy) on the northeast.

Diría National Park (Parque Nacional Diría, tel. 506/2680-1820, $10 entrance), covering 2,840 hectares of montane forests, including cloud forest, along the spine of the Nicoya mountains, lies 14 kilometers south of town. It has camping and trails.

Accommodations

A good deal is the motel-style **Hotel La Estancia** (tel./fax 506/2680-0476, $18 s or $25 d with fans, $23 s or $35 d with a/c), which has 15 pleasing modern units with fans, TVs, and private baths with hot water. Spacious family rooms have four beds. Some rooms are dark. There is secure parking.

Hotel La Rampa (tel. 506/2680-0586) competes and is similar.

Outshining all contenders is the **Hotel La Calle de Alcalá** (tel. 506/2680-0000, fax 506/2680-1633, $25 s, $40 d, $60 junior suite, $70 suite with whirlpool tub), one block south of Plaza de los Mangos. This Spanish-run hotel boasts a lively contempo decor and pleasing aesthetic. It has 29 air-conditioned rooms with cable TVs, bamboo furnishings, and pastels. They're set around an attractive swimming pool with swim-up bar. It has secure parking.

Food

For rustic ambience, try **Restaurante La Yunta** (tel. 506/2680-3031, 11 A.M.–11 P.M. Mon.–Sat., $2–10), facing Parque Ramos, in an old farmhouse-style building decorated in farm implements. It serves shrimp, lobster, octopus, and other seafood.

The most elegant restaurant in town is at **Hotel La Calle de Alcalá** (tel. 506/2680-0000, 7 A.M.–10 P.M.) serving *típico* dishes and seafood such as octopus in garlic ($8), plus filet mignon ($12). You'll also like **Casa Fonda** (tel. 506/2680-4949, 6 A.M.–10 P.M. Mon.–Sat., $2–10), facing Parque de los Mangos. Clean, modern, and open-air, this lovely spot serves ceviche ($3.50), soups, pastas, great seafood ($8), and even filet mignon ($9.50).

And the clean, modern **Ristorante Pizzería Da Giovanni** (tel. 2680-4128, 11 A.M.–10 P.M. Mon.–Sat.), on the main highway, will satisfy pizza cravings.

For baked goods, try **Musmanni,** 50 meters north of the main plaza.

Information and Services

MINAE (tel./fax 506/2680-1820 or 506/2680-1930, 8 A.M.–4 P.M. Mon.–Fri.) has a regional sub-office on the highway. However, it is not set up to assist tourists.

There are **banks** on Highway 21 at the entrance to town and on the north side of the main plaza. The **post office** is two blocks northeast of the main plaza.

The **Red Cross** is on the west side of the plaza. The **police station** (tel. 506/2680-0136) is on the northwest side of the bus station.

Cybermania (tel. 506/2680-4520, 8:30 A.M.–9:30 P.M. Mon.–Sat., 9 A.M.–8:30 P.M. Sun.), one block north of the main plaza, offers Internet service.

Getting There

Tracopa (tel. 506/2222-2666) buses depart

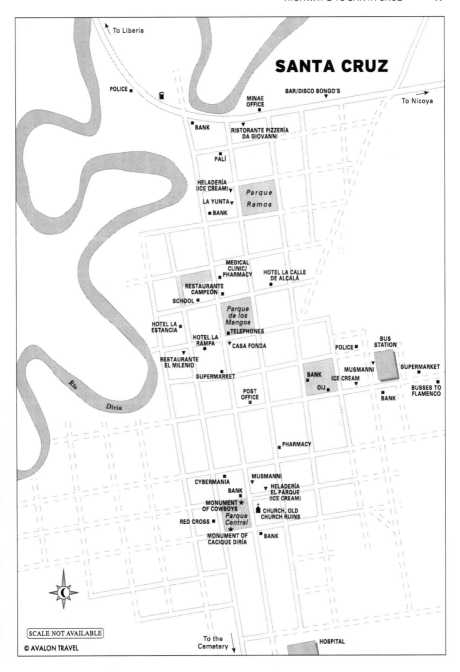

SANTA CRUZ

To Liberia

To Nicoya

POLICE

MINAE OFFICE

BAR/DISCO BONGO'S

BANK

RISTORANTE PIZZERÍA DA GIOVANNI

PALÍ

HELADERÍA (ICE CREAM)

Parque Ramos

LA YUNTA

BANK

MEDICAL CLINIC/ PHARMACY

HOTEL LA CALLE DE ALCALÁ

RESTAURANTE CAMPEÓN

SCHOOL

Parque de los Mangos

HOTEL LA ESTANCIA

TELEPHONES

HOTEL LA RAMPA

CASA FONDA

POLICE

BUS STATION

SUPERMARKET

RESTAURANTE EL MILENIO

SUPERMARKET

BANK

MUSMANNI ICE CREAM

BUSSES TO FLAMENCO

OIJ

BANK

POST OFFICE

Río

Diriá

PHARMACY

CYBERMANIA

MUSMANNI

BANK

HELADERÍA EL PARQUE (ICE CREAM)

MONUMENT OF COWBOYS

Parque Central

CHURCH, OLD CHURCH RUINS

RED CROSS

MONUMENT OF CACIQUE DIRÍA

BANK

SCALE NOT AVAILABLE

© AVALON TRAVEL

To the Cemetery

HOSPITAL

crafting traditional pottery at the Oven Store, Guaitíl

San José for Santa Cruz from Calle 14, Avenida 5 at 6:30 A.M., 10 A.M., 1:30 P.M., 3 P.M., and 5 P.M. daily ($5). Tralapa buses (tel. 506/2223-5859) depart San José for Santa Cruz from Calle 20, Avenidas 3/5, at seven times daily. Buses (tel. 506/665-5891) for Santa Cruz depart Liberia every 30 minutes 4:30 A.M.–8:30 P.M. (returning at the same time); from Nicoya hourly 6 A.M.–9 P.M. (returning at the same time); and from Puntarenas at 6 A.M. and 4 P.M. daily.

Tracopa buses depart Santa Cruz for San José at 3 A.M., 5 A.M., 6:30 A.M., 10:30 A.M., and 1:30 P.M. daily; Tralapa buses depart at 4:30 A.M., 5 A.M., 8:30 A.M., 11:30 A.M., and 5 P.M. daily.

Buses also depart Santa Cruz for Puntarenas, Playa Junquillal, Playa Flamingo, Playa Ostional, and Tamarindo.

◖ GUAITÍL

Guaitíl, 12 kilometers east of Santa Cruz (the turnoff from the main highway is two kilometers east of Santa Cruz), is a tranquil little village. Many of the inhabitants—descendants of Chorotegas—have been making their unique pottery of red or black or ocher using the same methods for generations, turning the clay on wheels and polishing the pottery with small jadelike grinding stones taken from nearby archaeological sites.

There are several artists' families, including in the adjacent village of San Vicente. (Every family seems to be attended by the matriarch: Women run the businesses and sustain families and village structures.) The women happily take you to the back of the house to see the large open-hearth kilns where the pots are fired.

Unfortunately, tour operators all stop at **Willy's,** because of the high commissions it pays, to the detriment of other retailers. If your tour bus stops here, move on to give other retailers a chance! My favorite place is the **Oven Store** (tel. 506/2681-1696, sjchlv@hotmail .com), where friendly owners Susan and Jesús offer five-hour pottery classes; it's on the northwest side of the soccer field.

The **Ecomuseo de la Cerámica Chorotega** (tel. 506/2681-1214, www.ecomuseodesan vicente.org), behind the school in San Vicente, was opened in 2007 to honor the local culture.

the author with a tapir at Tempisque Safari Ecological Adventure

Inspired by U.S. Peace Corps volunteers, it traces the ceramic tradition.

Getting There

Buses depart Santa Cruz for Guaitíl every two hours 7 A.M.–7 P.M. Mon.–Sat., 7 A.M.–2 P.M. Sunday. Hotels and tour companies throughout Nicoya also offer tours, as do some tour companies in San José.

PUERTO HUMO AND VICINITY

Puerto Humo is a small village on the west bank of the Río Tempisque, about 12 kilometers north of Barra Honda and most easily reached from the town of Nicoya (26 km). The bird-watching hereabouts is splendid. Puerto Humo is a gateway to Palo Verde National Park, across the river. **Aventuras Arenal** (tel. 506/2698-1142) offers boat trips ($45 pp with lunch).

The dirt road continues about five kilometers to the hamlet of Rosario, then peters out three kilometers farther along at the entrance (no facilities) to **Mata Redonda National Wildlife Refuge** (Refugio Nacional de Visa Silvestre Mata Redonda).

◖ Tempisque Safari Ecological Adventure

This fabulous facility (tel. 506/2698-1069, www.tempisquesafaricr.com, 10 A.M.–5 P.M. daily, $20 pp), hidden off the beaten track a kilometer beyond Rosario, is a total surprise and delight. Although part of a working cattle ranch, its highlight is the animal rescue and breeding center where snakes, monkeys, peccaries, tapirs, and cats such as the jaguarundi and margay are displayed in large cages. The crocodile lagoon is the real thing, and you'll be surprised to find yourself accompanied along the paths by free-strutting deer, rheas, and emus! There are even ostrich, capybara, and bison. A three-hour guided tour ($50 pp, minimum four people) is offered with a cart pulled by water buffalo, followed by a boat tour of the river. If the gates are closed, the *custodio* (guard) who lives opposite the entrance, will open up.

Getting There

A bus serves Puerto Humo twice daily, departing Nicoya township at 10 A.M., 3 P.M., and 6 P.M.

Playas del Coco and Vicinity

BAHÍA CULEBRA

Nicoya's most northerly beaches ring the horse-shoe-shaped Bahía Culebra (Snake Bay), enclosed to the north by the Nacascolo Peninsula, and to the south by the headland of Punta Ballena. The huge bay is a natural amphitheater rimmed by scarp cliffs cut with lonesome coves sheltering gray- and white-sand beaches and small mangrove swamps. There are remains of a pre-Columbian native settlement on the western shore of the bay at Nacascolo.

The north and south sides are approached separately by a pincer movement. The south side is reached via the road from Comunidad to Playa del Coco (the road divides two kilometers east of Playas del Coco; a turnoff leads three kilometers north to Playa Hermosa and, beyond Punta Ballena, to Playa Panamá). The north shore is reached from two kilometers north of Comunidad via a road immediately west of the Río Tempisque at Guardia. This road is a fast, sweeping, well-paved, lonesome beauty of a drive that dead-ends after 15 kilometers or so at the spectacular Four Seasons resort (no entry except to guests). En route you pass **Witch's Rock Canopy Tour** (tel. 506/2696-7101, http://witchsrockcanopytour.com, 8 A.M.–5 P.M. daily, last entry at 3:30 P.M.), 18 kilometers from Guardia. It has 23 platforms over a 2.5-kilometer course with four hanging bridges and even a tunnel ($55).

Marina Papagayo opened in December 2008 at Playa Manzanillo with 180 slips.

Playa Carbonal, immediately east of the bay, hosts the super-exclusive, members-only **Ellerstina Costa Rica Polo & Equestrian Beach Club** (tel. 506/2258-9219, http://ellerstinacr.com).

Accommodations

The **Occidental Allegro Papagayo** (tel. 506/2690-9900 or U.S. tel. 800/858-2258, www.occidental-hoteles.com, $286 s/d) overlooks Playa Manzanillo from a superb

THE GULF OF PAPAGAYO PROJECT

In 1993, the Costa Rican Tourism Institute (ICT) began to push roads into the hitherto inaccessible Nacascolo Peninsula. The government also leased 2,000 hectares surrounding the bay as part of the long-troubled Gulf of Papagayo Tourism Project of the ICT, begun in 1974 but left to languish until a few years ago, when development suddenly took off exponentially with the enthusiastic backing of the Rafael Calderón administration. The mini-Cancún that began to emerge was intended to push Costa Rica into the big leagues of resort tourism.

Headed by Grupo Papagayo, a conglomerate of independent companies headed by Mexico's Grupo Situr, the 88-kilometer-long coastal concession was planned as a 15-year development. Developers and environmentalists squared off over the project. An independent review panel expressed concern about illegal activities and environmental degradation. In March 1995, the former tourism minister and 12 other senior ICT officials were indicted as charges of corruption began to fly.

The Nacascolo Peninsula is an area of archaeological importance with many pre-Columbian sites. When it was discovered that bulldozers were plowing heedlessly, the government issued an executive decree to declare the peninsula a place of historic importance. To improve its image, the Grupo changed the name of the project to Ecodesarollo Papagayo, or Papagayo Eco-Development. Then the company went bankrupt, bursting the Papagayo bubble. The bulldozers remained idle. In 1999, North American investors took over and more conscientious development resulted in the opening, in 2004, of the Four Seasons Papagayo resort. Development is ongoing.

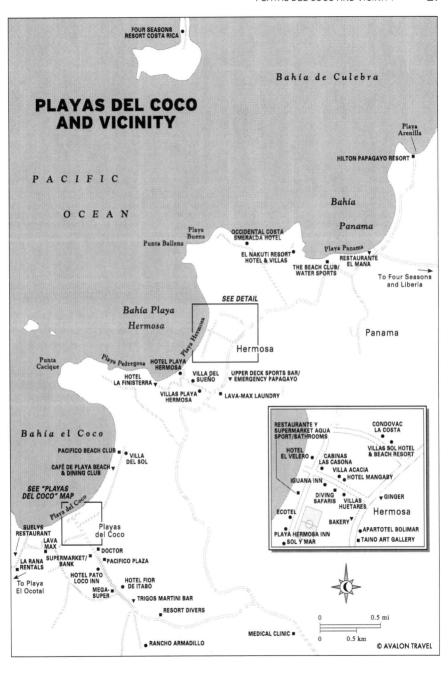

FOUR SEASONS
RESORT COSTA RICA •

Bahía de Culebra

PLAYAS DEL COCO
AND VICINITY

Playa
Arenilla

HILTON PAPAGAYO RESORT ■

P A C I F I C

Bahía

O C E A N

Panama

Playa
Buena

OCCIDENTAL COSTA
SMERALDA HOTEL

Punta Ballena

Playa Panama

EL NAKUTI RESORT
HOTEL & VILLAS

RESTAURANTE
EL MANA

THE BEACH CLUB/
WATER SPORTS

To Four Seasons
and Liberia

SEE DETAIL

Bahía Playa

Panama

Hermosa

Hermosa

Punta
Cacique

Playa Pedregosa

HOTEL PLAYA
HERMOSA

HOTEL
LA FINISTERRA ▼

VILLA DEL
SUEÑO

UPPER DECK SPORTS BAR/
▼ EMERGENCY PAPAGAYO

VILLAS PLAYA
HERMOSA

■ LAVA-MAX LAUNDRY

Bahía el Coco

PACIFICO BEACH CLUB ■

■ VILLA
DEL SOL

CAFÉ DE PLAYA BEACH ▼
& DINING CLUB

**SEE "PLAYAS
DEL COCO" MAP**

Playas
del Coco

SUELYS
RESTAURANT
LAVA
MAX

LA RANA ■
RENTALS

SUPERMARKET/
BANK

■ DOCTOR

■ PACIFICO PLAZA

To Playa
El Ocotal

HOTEL PATO
LOCO INN

MEGA-
SUPER

HOTEL FIOR
DE ITABO

■ TRIGOS MARTINI BAR

RESORT DIVERS ■

MEDICAL CLINIC ■

■ RANCHO ARMADILLO

RESTAURANTE Y
SUPERMARKET AQUA
SPORT/BATHROOMS

CONDOVAC
LA COSTA

VILLAS SOL HOTEL
& BEACH RESORT

HOTEL
EL VELERO

CABINAS
LAS CASONA

VILLA ACACIA

IGUANA INN

■ HOTEL MANGABY

DIVING
SAFARIS

VILLAS
HUETARES

▼ GINGER

ECOTEL

Hermosa

BAKERY ▼

PLAYA HERMOSA INN

■ APARTOTEL BOLIMAR

■ SOL Y MAR

■ TAINO ART GALLERY

0   0.5 mi

0   0.5 km

© AVALON TRAVEL

© CHRISTOPHER P. BAKER

Hilton Papagayo Resort

breeze-swept hillside perch. This four-star, all-inclusive resort has 308 graciously appointed air-conditioned rooms in three-story edifices stair-stepping the hillside. Action centers on the huge pool with swim-up bar. A theater hosts shows, and there's a disco and sports bar, plus water sports and scuba. Alas, the paltry gray-sand beach holds little attraction. In February 2008 the hotel was temporarily shut down by the Ministry of Health for pumping raw sewage into the estuary.

The super-deluxe ⟨ **Four Seasons Resort Costa Rica at Peninsula Papagayo** (tel. 506/2696-0500, www.fourseasons.com/costarica, from $675 s/d low season, from $815 s/d high season), at the tip of Punta Mala, brought a whole new panache to the region when it opened in 2004, with 145 spacious guest rooms, including 25 suites, exuding luxury, fine taste, and every amenity you could hope for. Facilities include a gorgeous spa and Arnold Palmer–designed 18-hole golf course (open to resort guests only). The setting is sublime, with two distinct beaches to each side (one bayside, the other shelving into the Pacific ocean).

A super-deluxe **Fairmont** is also planned, with a marina and new golf course. **Mandarin Oriental** is slated to open a deluxe hotel, and the equally sumptuous 120-room **Regent Resort at La Punta Papagayo** (www.regenthotels.com) is expected to open by 2010 with a world-class spa and massive retail village. And at last visit, ground was to be broken on the **Condohotel Casa Conde del Mar** (www.casacondedelmar.com) at Playa Chorotega.

PLAYA HERMOSA AND PLAYA PANAMÁ

Playa Hermosa, separated from Playa del Coco to the south by Punta Cacique and from Bahía Culebra to the north by Punta Ballena, is a pleasant two-kilometer-wide, curving gray-sand beach with good tidepools at its northern end. The road continues one kilometer to Playa Panamá, a narrow, two-kilometers-wide gray-sand beach in a cove bordered by low, scrub-covered hills—a bay within a bay. The beach is popular with Ticos, who camp along it. Weekends and holidays get crowded.

The road dead-ends atop the headland overlooking **Playa Arenilla** and Bahía Culebra.

The much-troubled **Cacique del Mar** residential project atop Punta Cacique has been resurrected and is slated to host two five-star boutique hotels.

Entertainment

Villas del Sueño has live bands three nights weekly in high season, plus guest appearances in low season. Sports fans might check out the charmless, overly air-conditioned **Upperdeck Bar** (tel. 506/2672-1276, 9 A.M.–2 A.M. daily).

Tours and Activities

Diving Safaris (tel. 506/2672-1259, www.costaricadiving.net) has daily two-tank dive trips ($65), night and Nitrox dives, and certification courses. Snorkelers can accompany dive boats ($30). **Resort Divers de Costa Rica** (tel. 506/2670-0421, www.resortdivers-cr.com) offers surfing trips and sportfishing as well as snorkeling and scuba trips.

Aqua Sport (tel. 506/2670-0050, samaci@racsa.co.cr) offers all manner of water sports, plus boat tours and fishing. And **Velas de Papagayo** (tel. 506/2223-2508, www.velasdepapagayo.com, $100 pp) has snorkeling, sunset, and nighttime sailing trips out of Playa Panamá, where **Water Sports** (tel. 506/2672-0012) has water-skiing and personal watercraft.

Accommodations

CAMPING

You can camp at **Restaurante El Mama,** 200 meters inland of the beach at Playa Panamá.

$25-50

The no-frills **Iguana Inn** (tel. 506/2672-0065, $20 s, $30 d), in the heart of Hermosa, is a popular surf camp with 10 simple rooms with private bathrooms in a two-story wooden lodge 100 meters from the beach. Its Jammin' Restaurant is a popular spot.

Nearby, backpackers might try the German-owned **Cabinas Las Casona** (tel. 506/2672-0025, $28 s/d low season, $38 s/d high season), an old home that has eight simple but clean rooms with fans, small kitchenettes, and private baths with cold water.

$50-100

Nearby, the modern **Hotel ManGaby** (tel. 506/2672-0048, www.hotelmangaby.com, $72 s/d standard, $94 mini-suite, $172 suite low season; $102 s/d standard, $118 mini-suite, $197 suite high season) is a perfectly adequate option in the mid-price category, with pleasantly furnished rooms and a swimming pool.

Directly overlooking Playa Hermosa, **Hotel El Velero** (tel. 506/2672-1017, www.costaricahotel.net, $75 s/d low season, $89 high season) is an intimate Spanish colonial-style hostelry with 22 modestly appointed, air-conditioned rooms (some also have fans). The hotel has both upstairs and downstairs restaurants open to the breezes, plus a boutique and a small pool surrounded by shady palms. The hotel offers tours and scuba diving.

At the south end of Hermosa, you can't go wrong at the splendid Canadian-run **Villa del Sueño** (tel. 506/2672-0026 or U.S. tel. 800/378-8599, www.villadelsueno.com, $65 s/d standard, $89 superior, $109 junior suite low season; $75 s/d standard, $105 superior, $130 junior suite high season), an exquisite Spanish colonial-style building offering six air-conditioned rooms in the main house and eight rooms in two two-story, whitewashed stone buildings surrounding a lushly landscaped courtyard with a swimming pool. The rooms boast terra-cotta tiled floors, lofty hardwood ceilings with fans, large picture windows, contemporary artwork, beautiful batik fabrics, bamboo furniture, and pastels. The gourmet restaurant hosts live music.

Also to consider are the charming **Villa Acacia** (tel. 506/2672-1000, www.villacacia.com), with eight villas and a swimming pool; the upscale self-catering **Villas Playa Hermosa** (tel. 506/2672-1239, www.villasplayhermosa.com); the less impressive **Playa Hermosa Inn** (tel. 506/2672-0050, fax 506/2672-0060); and, if you're seeking a self-catering option, **Hotel & Villas Huetares** (tel. 506/2672-0052, www.villahuetares.com, $45 s/d room, $80 s/d villa low season; $80 s/d room, $135 s/d villa high season), an apartment-style complex of 15 two-bedroom bungalows in lush grounds.

The large-scale **Condovac La Costa** (tel. 506/2527-4000, www.condovac.com, from $75 s, $95 d, including breakfast) commands the hill at the northern end of the beach and appeals mainly to Ticos. It offers 101 air-conditioned villas, plus there's a selection of bars and restaurants, a full complement of tours, sportfishing, and scuba diving.

The former Costa Blanca del Pacifico is now the **Monarch Resort Hotel** (tel. 506/2672-1363, www.monarchresortonline.com, $109 s/d low season, $149 s/d high season), with suites furnished in elegant contemporary fashion. Its lofty perch atop the headland guarantees fine vistas.

$100-150

Another winner is the bargain-priced, Canadian-owned **Hotel La Finisterra** (tel. 506/2670-0227, www.lafinisterra.com, $90 s/d low season, $110 s/d high season), a handsome contemporary structure atop the breezy headland at the south end of the beach. What views! The 10 simply furnished yet delightful air-conditioned rooms boast fans, attractive bamboo furniture, and wide, screened windows; some have forest (not beach) views. The open-sided restaurant looks over a charming irregular-shaped swimming pool. The owners have a 38-foot sailboat ($60 for a full-day tour); sportfishing tours are arranged. Rates include full breakfast.

For an all-inclusive bargain consider **El Nakuti Resort Hotel & Villas** (tel. 506/2672-1212, www.nakutiresort.com, $75 s or $120 d low season, $95 s or $150 d high season), a handsome modern property with 97 rooms in thatched air-conditioned chalets arrayed in the style of an indigenous village in landscaped grounds. Sponge-washed walls in warm ocher shades enhance the mood. Each bungalow has a separate living room with kitchen. There's a large pool and kids' pool. It has sea kayaks, snorkeling, water-skiing, sunset cruises, plus mountain bike and ATV rentals. Rates include tax.

$150-200

Wearing an exciting new livery, **❮ Hotel Playa Hermosa** (tel./fax 506/2672-0046, www.hotelplayahermosa.com, $125 s/d junior suite, $150–175 suites low season; $175 s/d junior suite, $225–275 suites high season), at the southern end of the beach, has been turned into the class act in Playa Hermosa. Still in the works at last visit, the new twin-level suites are built around a gorgeous walk-in swimming pool and half-moon wooden sundeck shaded by a giant *guanacaste* tree. Designed with a graceful Balinese motif, the rooms have their own balconies overlooking the pool. It will have 38 junior suites when complete, and at last visit the old beachfront standard rooms were in the midst of being replaced by six smashing new rooms in a three-story tower with new restaurant and lounge-bar.

If all-inclusive resort elegance is your thing, **Villas Sol Hotel & Beach Resort** (tel. 506/2257-067, www.villassol.com, $574 standard, $828 one-bedroom villa for two nights minimum), next to Condovac La Costa, has 54 deluxe hotel rooms and 106 attractive villas (24 with private pools) recently refurbished in fashionably contemporary vogue, including flat-screen TVs, and modern amenities. There's a swimming pool, three restaurants, and a disco, and water sports and other activities are included.

OVER $200

At Playa Buena, the beautiful and expansive all-inclusive **Occidental Gran Papagayo** (tel. 506/2672-0193, www.occidental-hoteles.com, $392 s/d high season) draws a mostly Tico clientele. The 169 beautiful, air-conditioned bungalows (with seven types of rooms) stair-step down grassy lawns. Hardwoods and terra-cotta tiles abound. Plate-glass walls and doors proffer priceless vistas. Suites have mezzanine bedrooms and king-size beds, plus deep sea-green marble in the bathrooms, which have whirlpool tubs. It has two restaurants and a large pool set like a jewel on the slopes. There's a tennis court and shops, plus scuba diving and tours. Call for varying rates.

Sensational! That's the term for the marvelously situated **◖ Hilton Papagayo Resort** (tel. 506/2672-0000, www.hilton.com, from $369 s/d), a sprawling all-inclusive with 202 rooms, suites, and bungalows nestled on the scarp face overlooking Playa Arenilla, immediately north of Playa Panamá. This remarkable remake of the former Fiesta resort is stylish and sophisticated, beginning in the open-air lobby that offers tantalizing views over the bay. Its infinity pool and handsome use of thatch are pluses, as are the gorgeous bedrooms with sophisticated contemporary styling, quality linens, flat-screen TVs, in-room safes, and other modern conveniences. Three restaurants include an Italian open-air dining room under soaring thatch, the thatched beachfront grill, and the chic La Consecha, serving gourmet fusion fare. There's a great spa.

Westin plans to build a super-deluxe hotel. And the deluxe **Miraval Life in Balance** and **One and Only** boutique hotels are planned for Cacique del Mar.

Food

For simple surrounds on the sands, head to **Restaurant Valle's Mar** (tel. 506/8896-3694, 10 A.M.–9 P.M.). It serves hearty seafood dishes, such as ceviche, fried calamari ($8), and grilled mahimahi with garlic ($8).

The best food for miles is served at **◖ Ginger** (tel. 506/2672-0041, 5–10 P.M. Tues.–Sun., $5–20), beside the main road in the heart of Hermosa. This chic and contemporary tapas bar is run by Canadian chef Anne Hegney Frey. Striking for its minimalist design, with a trapezoidal bar, walls of glass, and cantilevered glass roof, it also delivers fantastic food. Try the ginger rolls, fried calamari, or superb ginger ahi tuna. Two-for-one sushi rolls are served 5–10 P.M. Friday. My martini was ridiculously small for the price, however.

I also recommend **Villas del Sueño** hotel restaurant (tel. 506/2672-0026), where the rotating daily menu may include scallopini parmesan, tenderloin with brandy and three-pepper sauce, mahimahi with shrimp and cream sauce ($15.50), and profiteroles ($5–13).

Elegant place settings, low lighting, and mellow music enhance the atmosphere. It does special dinners.

Similarly, **The Bistro** (tel. 506/2670-0227, 10 A.M.–10 P.M. daily), at Hotel Finisterra, is open to the public, with a creative French chef conjuring Caesar salad ($3.50), filet mignon with peppercorn sauce ($10), and daily pastas. Friday is sushi night. It earns rave reviews and draws diners from afar.

Restaurante Aqua Sport (tel. 506/2672-0050, 9 A.M.–9 P.M.) has a pleasing thatched beachfront restaurant at Playa Hermosa, with crepes, ceviche, salads, and a wide-ranging seafood menu.

Information and Services

Aqua Sport has a public telephone, souvenir shop, and general store (6 A.M.–9 P.M. daily). The **Emergencias Papagayo** (tel. 506/2670-0047) medical clinic is on the main road, alongside **Lavandería Lava Max** (tel. 506/2672-0136) laundry; and **Lavandería Bolimar** (8 A.M.–5 P.M. Mon.–Fri.) 100 meters farther north. Villa Acacia (tel. 506/2672-1000, www.villacacia.com) has an Internet café.

Getting There

A bus departs San José for Playa Hermosa and Panamá from Calle 20, Avenidas 1/3, daily at 3:25 P.M. (five hours). Buses depart Liberia for Playa Hermosa seven times daily, 5:30 A.M.–7:30 P.M. Buses depart Hermosa for San José at 5:10 A.M., and for Liberia seven times daily 6:10 A.M.–7:10 P.M.

A taxi from Coco will run about $5 one-way; from Liberia about $15.

PLAYAS DEL COCO

Playas del Coco, 35 kilometers west of Liberia, is one of the most accessible beach resorts in Guanacaste. The place can be crowded during weekends and holidays, when Josefinos flock. A two-kilometer-wide gray-sand beach (it is referred to in the plural—Playas del Coco) lines the horseshoe-shaped bay. Coco is still an active fishing village; the touristy area is to the east, and the laid-back fishing village is to the west.

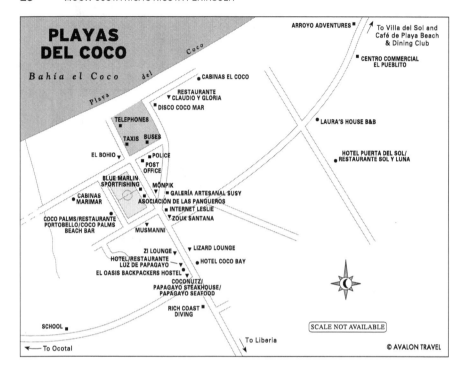

Playas del Coco is also a center for scuba diving.

The past few years have seen an incredible boom in real estate development. Meanwhile, in 2008 the local municipality bulldozed much of the shorefront property, which as a boon opened up more of the beach to view. At last visit, construction of the **Marina Punta Cacique** was slated to begin in 2009.

Entertainment and Events

Coco is a lively spot and hosts a five-day *fiesta cívica* in late January, with bullfights, rodeos, and folkloric dancing.

The most-fun spot is the open-air **Coconutz Sports Bar** (tel. 506/2670-1981, http://coconutz-cr.com), which shows alfresco movies on a big screen and has live music on Friday, Saturday, and Monday. It serves pizza and Tex-Mex.

The **Lizard Lounge** (tel. 506/2670-0307, www.lizardloungecr.com) has a pool table, plus a happy hour 5–7 P.M. daily. Wednesday

is Italian night; Thursday is Ladies Night; and you're offered $2 shots Friday and Saturday.

The tiny, Italian-run **Zouk Santana** (tel. 506/2670-0191, www.zouksantana.com, 7:30 A.M.–11:30 A.M. daily) is a sophisticated spot for supping and enjoying a cigar, sold on-site. The same owners run the hip **Café de Playa** (tel. 506/2670-1621, www.cafedeplaya.com, 7 A.M.–midnight daily), a beach club where a DJs spin tunes and special theme parties are hosted.

The hip new **Tragos Martini Bar,** scheduled to open at last visit, also reflects the area's increasingly upscale trend. And the **Coco Palms Beach Bar** (2–9 P.M.), on the west side of the soccer field, is a nice spot for a quiet drink.

Later at night, the budget crowd and locals gravitate to the **Disco Coco Mar** (tel. 506/2670-0358), a no-frills disco on Saturday, and karaoke other nights.

Gamblers can try their hand with Lady Luck

at the small **casinos** in Hotel Flor de Itabo (506/2670-0290, 8 P.M.–2 A.M. daily).

Tours and Activities

The **Asociación de las Pangueros** (tel. 506/2670-0228, rocasurf@hotmail.com), the local fishermen's association, offers boats and guide services.

Rich Coast Diving (tel./fax 506/2670-0176, www.richcoastdiving.com) has a full-service dive center, plus a 35-foot trimaran for charter. **Summer Salt Dive Center** (tel. 506/2670-0308, www.summer-salt.com) also has snorkel rental plus dive trips. **Coco Sea Sport** (tel. 506/2670-1514, www.cocoseasport.com) has personal watercraft rental, yacht charter, and snorkeling.

A fun day trip is to cruise the local beaches with **Arroyo Adventures** (tel. 506/2670-0239, www.grupomapache.com), which also offers sportfishing.

Hacienda Chapernal (tel. 506/2273-4545, www.elchapernal.com), four kilometers southeast of Sardinal, is a working cattle ranch offering horseback riding, plus folkloric music and dance.

Accommodations

UNDER $25

Backpackers give a thumbs up to **El Oasis Backpackers Hostel** (tel. 506/2670-0501, www.eloasiscostarica.com, $13 pp low season, $15 pp high season), new in 2008 and tucked behind Papagayo Steak House in a garden with hammocks beneath palms. It has three spacious air-conditioned dorms with ceiling fans and modern bathrooms. It has a communal kitchen, lockers, and a pleasant TV lounge with Internet, plus DVD library, a laundry, and bikes and snorkeling gear for rent.

The **Cabinas Marimar** (tel. 506/2670-1212, $15 pp), facing the beach, has 17 no-frills rooms with fans and private baths with cold water only.

$25-50

The ever-evolving **Coco Palms** (tel. 506/2670-0367, www.hotelcocopalms.com, $35–60 s/d rooms, $80–150 apartments low season; call for high season rates), on the west side of the soccer field, offers 48 spacious, adequately furnished air-conditioned rooms arrayed along an atrium corridor, all with fans, cable TV, and Wi-Fi. Some have whirlpool tubs and kitchens or kitchenettes. There's a lap pool and the delightful Restaurante Coco Sushi.

The pleasing, Italian-run **Hotel Pato Loco Inn** (tel./fax 506/670-0145, patoloco@racsa.co.cr, $35 s/d with fan, $45 with a/c low season; $40 s/d with fan, $50 with a/c high season), 800 meters inland on the main drag, has attractive rooms—three triples, one double, and two fully equipped apartments—with orthopedic mattresses, central air-conditioning, and modest furnishings with hardwood accents. There's a small but quality Italian restaurant.

New in 2008, and also to consider in this price bracket, is **Hotel Luz de Papagayo** (tel. 506/2670-0400, fax 506/2670-0319), with six nicely furnished upstairs rooms.

$50-100

The beachfront **Cabinas El Coco** (tel. 506/2670-0230, fax 506/2670-0276, cabinaselcoco@racsa.co.cr, $50 s/d low season, $100 s/d high season) has been remodeled but remains unimpressive and is now ridiculously overpriced.

Laura's House B&B (tel. 506/2670-0751, www.laurashousecr.net, $50 s, $60 d) is run by a delightful young Tica and offers seven lovely albeit simply furnished air-conditioned rooms in a two-story house, all with ceiling fans and clean private bathrooms. Downstairs rooms are pleasingly cool; some have bunks. There's a pool in the courtyard with hammocks, plus Wi-Fi and parking.

Farther east, the **Villa del Sol** (tel. 506/8301-8848, www.villadelsol.com, $45–50 s, $55–65 d low season; $50–65 s, $65–75 d high season), set amid lawns, is a homey bed-and-breakfast with an open atrium lounge. Seven air-conditioned rooms vary considerably, though all have ceiling fans and simple decor blessed with lively colors. Five have private bathrooms and balconies plus king-size bed. It also offers six new studio apartments.

There's a swimming pool and whirlpool tub. It has secure parking.

I love **《 Hotel Puerta del Sol** (tel. 506/2670-0195, fax 506/2670-0650, no website, $45 s or $65 d standard, $85 suites low season; $55 s or $85 d standard, $110 suites high season), an intimate hotel with an Italian aesthetic. The 10 whitewashed air-conditioned rooms (with tropical pastels in counterpoint) feature soft-contoured walls enveloping king-size beds and melding into wraparound sofas built into the walls. All have ceiling fans, TVs, phones, safes, fridges, coffeemakers, and patios. Two are suites with refrigerators, and *casitas* have full kitchens. A small airy lounge has games and a TV, and there's a garden with a charming lap pool and gym. The restaurant excels. Free scuba lessons are offered in the pool. Rates include breakfast.

Sportfishing fans should head to **Hotel Flor de Itabo** (tel. 506/2670-0290, www.florde itabo.com, $55 s or $65 d standard, $85–105 s/d deluxe, $145 villas low season; $70 s or $85 d standard, $105–135 s/d deluxe, $145 villas high season), about one kilometer before Coco. It has 10 spacious standard rooms, seven deluxe rooms with whirlpool tubs, and eight bungalow apartments. The Sailfish Restaurant opens onto a pool in landscaped grounds full of parrots and macaws. There's also a casino. The hotel specializes in fishing trips.

For peaceful seclusion, I recommend **Rancho Armadillo** (tel. 506/2670-0108, www.ranchoarmadillo.com, $100–146 s/d low season, $145–200 high season). This beautiful Spanish-colonial-style hacienda, on a 10-hectare hillside *finca* 1.5 kilometers from the beach, has six spacious air-conditioned bungalows, including a two-bedroom suite. All have fans, magnificent hardwood furniture, wrought-iron balustrades, lofty wooden ceilings, hardwood floors, colorful Guatemalan bedspreads, stained-glass windows, "rainforest" showers, coffeemakers, refrigerators, and cable TV. There's also a house for families or groups, plus an open-air kitchen beside the swimming pool, a gym, a *mirador* lounge with hammocks and rockers, and a library. Meals are offered

by request. The estate is available for exclusive rental during peak season, with Rick, the owner, as chef (he was for years a professional chef). Rates include breakfast.

My favorite place to relax is the **《 Café de Playa Beach & Dining Club** (tel. 506/2670-1621, www.cafedeplaya.com, $160 s/d low season, $200 s/d high season), a chic club with a circular swimming pool and "parachute" canopy over wooden sundeck and open-air sushi bar, plus lounge chairs on the beachfront lawn. It has a Hobie Cat and yacht. This hip conversion of the former Hotel Vista Mar has five totally remodeled rooms with a super contemporary aesthetic fitting for Manhattan or Beverly Hills. Each of the suites is distinct. And divine!

Food

Papagayo Steakhouse & Seafood (tel. 506/2670-0298, noon–10 P.M.) is a two-in-one restaurant: an open-air seafood restaurant downstairs and an air-conditioned one serving meats upstairs. The seafood menu includes sashimi and blackened Cajun-style catch of the day ($8–15). It also sells fresh fish at a streetside outlet.

Restaurante Coco Sushi (tel. 506/2670-0367, 11 A.M.–11 P.M. daily), on the west side of the soccer field, is a modestly elegant eatery with a creative menu featuring sautéed black tip shark, curry shrimp stir fry, and sushi and Japanese fare.

For prize Italian fare, head to **Restaurante Sol y Luna** (5–10 P.M. Wed.–Mon.) at Hotel Puerta del Sol; it serves homemade pastas ($5), cannelloni ($7.50), lasagna ($8), stuffed crepes, tiramisu, and daily specials, enjoyed amid exquisite Romanesque decor. It also serves cappuccinos and espressos, and has a large wine list and 15 types of beer.

If you want a truly classy ambience by the beach, check out **Café de Playa Beach & Dining Club** (tel. 506/2670-1621, www.cafede playa.com, 7 A.M.–midnight daily, $5–20). It serves great breakfasts and has a sushi bar, and the classy breeze-swept restaurant serves everything from salads and penne pastas to nouvelle seafood such as rum-sauce jumbo shrimp. In a similar vein, the beachfront **Restaurant Claudio y Gloria** (tel. 506/3670-1514, www.cocoseasport.com) competes with elegant place settings and an eclectic menu featuring ceviche, mahimahi with leek sauce ($13), and Peruvian dishes.

The tops in elegant dining, however, is the **Restaurant Pacifico Beach Club** (tel. 506/2670-2212, www.pacifico-costarica.com, 11 A.M.–3 P.M. daily, and 6–10 P.M. Fri.–Sun.), with a stately contemporary motif that includes an onyx-topped bar with flat-screen TVs. It serves tapas and Häagen-Daz ice cream.

Less pretentious, and my favorite place, is **(Suely's Restaurant** (tel. 506/2670-1696, sti-costarica@hotmail.com, 11:30 A.M.–11 P.M. daily), one kilometer west of town. Run by two French sisters, it has a lovely ambience, with multitiered decks beneath shade trees. The changing menu might include tuna tartare ($5), gazpacho ($4), pan-seared brie ($6), crusted salmon ($7), and a seafood selection with jumbo shrimp, mussels, scallops and rice with saffron sauce on a bed of leek fondue. Leave room for the chocolate volcano.

Craving a cappuccino and a brownie sundae? Head to **Coco Coffee Co.** (tel. 506/2670-1055, 7 A.M.–4 P.M. Mon.–Sat.). It also has bagels, fruit plates, and salads.

Information and Services

The **post office** (8 A.M.–noon and 2–5:30 P.M. Mon.–Fri.) and **police station** (tel. 506/2670-0258) face the plaza, which has public telephones.

There's a **medical clinic** (tel. 506/2670-0047) about three kilometers east of town. The **Red Cross** (tel. 506/2670-0190) is in Sardinal, eight kilometers east of Playas del Coco.

For Internet, I use **Internet Leslie** (tel. 506/2670-0156, 8 A.M.–10 P.M. Mon.–Sat., 2–10 P.M. Sun.).

Lava Max (tel. 506/2670-1860, 8 A.M.–6 P.M. Mon.–Sat.) is the place to do laundry.

Getting There and Around

Pulmitan buses (tel. 506/2222-1650) depart San José for Playas del Coco from Avenida 5, Calles 24, daily at 8 A.M., 2 P.M., and 4 P.M. ($5.50, five hours), returning at 4 A.M., 8 A.M., and 2 P.M. Buses depart Liberia (Arata, tel. 506/2666-0138), for Coco eight times daily.

Interbus (tel. 506/2283-5573, www.inter busonline.com) operates minibus shuttles from San José ($35) and popular tourist destinations in Nicoya and Guanacaste.

Taxis (tel. 506/2670-0303) park by the plaza.

There's a gas station in Sardinal. **Adobe Rent-a-Car** (tel. 506/8811-4242, www.adobe car.com) has an office in Pacifico Plaza, and you can rent scooters at **La Rana Rentals** (tel. 506/2670-1312).

PLAYA EL OCOTAL

This secluded gray-sand beach is three kilometers southwest of Playa del Coco within the cusp of steep cliffs. It's smaller and more secluded than Coco, but it gets the overflow on busy weekends. The rocky headlands at each end have tidepools. Ocotal is a base for sportfishing and scuba diving. At Las Corridas, a dive spot only a kilometer from Ocotal, divers are sure of coming face-to-face with massive jewfish, which make this rock reef their home; black marlin are occasionally seen.

Ocotal Diving Safaris (tel. 506/2670-0321 ext. 120, www.ocotaldiving.com) rents equipment and offers various dive trips, including a free introductory dive daily, plus snorkeling. It also offers deep-sea fishing ($425 half day, $645 full day up to four people).

Accommodations

The bay is dominated by **El Ocotal Beach Resort & Marina** (tel. 506/2670-0321, www .ocotalresort.com, $120 s or $162 d standard, $241 s/d junior suite, $283 s/d suite low season; $157 s or $180 d standard, $278 s/d junior suite, $341 s/d suite high season), a gleaming whitewashed structure that stair-steps up the cliffs at the southern end of the beach. It has 71 attractive air-conditioned rooms with fans, freezers, two queen-size beds each, satellite TVs, direct-dial telephones, and ocean views. The original 12 rooms are in six duplex

Playa el Ocotal

bungalows; newer rooms have their own whirl-pool tub, sunning area, and pool. Three small pools each have *ranchitos* for shade, and there are tennis courts and horseback riding, plus a fully equipped dive shop, sportfishing boats, and car rental.

Hotel Villa Casa Blanca (tel. 506/2670-448, www.hotelvillacasablanca.com, $85 s/d standard, $105 s/d suite low season; $195 s/d standard, $125 s/d suite high season) sets a standard for beachside bed-and-breakfasts, although at last visit the public structures were deteriorating. The upscale Spanish-style villa is set in a lush landscaped garden full of yuccas and bougainvillea. The small swimming pool has a swim-up bar and a sundeck with lounge chairs. Inside, the hotel epitomizes subdued elegance with its intimate allure: sponge-washed walls, four-poster beds (six rooms), stenciled murals, and massive bathrooms with deep tubs and wall-to-wall mirrors. The 14 rooms include four suites (two are honeymoon suites). You can relax in a whirlpool tub, and there's a patio restaurant and grill.

Food

The rustic and offbeat beachfront **❰ Father Rooster Restaurant** (tel. 506/2670-1246, 11 A.M.–10 P.M. daily, $2–10) run by Steve, a friendly Floridian, is the hip, happening place to be. It serves seafood dishes, quesadillas, burgers, and Caesar salads, plus huge margaritas ($4.50). It has a sand volleyball court, pool table, darts, and occasional live music.

If you're feeling flush, try the cuisine at **El Ocotal Beach Resort** (tel. 506/2670-0321, www.ocotalresort.com), which one reader raves about.

Playa Flamingo and Vicinity

South of Playas del Coco are Playa Flamingo and a series of contiguous beaches accessed by paved road via the communities of **Portegolpe** and **Huacas** (reached from Hwy. 21 via Belén, 8 km south of Filadelfia). At Huacas, you turn right for Playas Brasilito, Flamingo, Potrero, Penca, and Azucar, where the road ends. If you don't turn right, the road keeps straight for **Matapalo,** where you turn right for Playa Conchal, and left for Playa Grande.

The "Monkey Trail"

A more direct route from Playas del Coco is via a dirt road—the "Monkey Trail"—that begins three kilometers east of Playa del Coco and one kilometer west of Sardinal and leads

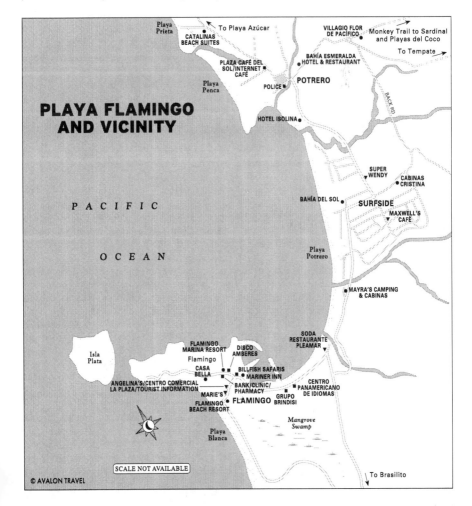

PLAYA FLAMINGO
AND VICINITY

PACIFIC

OCEAN

Playa Prieta

To Playa Azúcar

CATALINAS BEACH SUITES

PLAZA CAFÉ DEL SOL/INTERNET CAFÉ

Playa Penca

POLICE

VILLAGIO FLOR DE PACÍFICO

Monkey Trail to Sardinal and Playas del Coco

To Tempate

BAHÍA ESMERALDA HOTEL & RESTAURANT

POTRERO

BACK RD

HOTEL ISOLINA

SUPER WENDY

CABINAS CRISTINA

BAHÍA DEL SOL

SURFSIDE

MAXWELL'S CAFÉ

Playa Potrero

MAYRA'S CAMPING & CABINAS

Isla Plata

FLAMINGO MARINA RESORT

Flamingo

CASA BELLA

ANGELINA'S/CENTRO COMERCIAL LA PLAZA/TOURIST INFORMATION

MARIE'S

FLAMINGO BEACH RESORT

DISCO AMBERES

BILLFISH SAFARIS

MARINER INN

BANK/CLINIC/ PHARMACY

FLAMINGO

SODA RESTAURANTE PLEAMAR

CENTRO PANAMERICANO DE IDIOMAS

GRUPO BRINDISI

Mangrove Swamp

Playa Blanca

SCALE NOT AVAILABLE

© AVALON TRAVEL

To Brasilito

to Potrero. It can be rough going in wet season. About nine kilometers southwest from Sardinal is the **Congo Trail Canopy Tour** (tel. 506/2666-4422, congotrail@racsa.co.cr, 8 A.M.–5 P.M. daily), where for $35 you can whiz between treetop platforms on a zipline, granting a monkey's-eye view with the howler (congo) monkeys. It also has a butterfly farm, serpentarium, monkeys, and an aviary.

When passing through Portegolpe, consider a quick stop at the **Monkey Park** (tel. 506/2653-8060, www.monkey-park.org, 8 A.M.–4 P.M. Tues.–Sun., $5), an animal rescue center that takes in injured and confiscated monkeys that cannot survive in the wild. You'll also see peccaries, coati, deer, caimans, and lots of birds. It has a breeding program and accepts visitors for a one-hour guided tour ($15). Nearby, **Cartagena Canopy Tour** (tel. 506/2675-4501, www.canopytourcartagena.com, $35 pp) lets you whiz through the treetops. It has tours at 8 A.M., 11 A.M., 1 P.M., and 3 P.M. by reservation. Free hotel transfers are offered.

Horse-riding anyone? Head to **Haras del Mar Equestrian Center** (tel. 506/8820-0474, www.lomasdelmar.com), midway along the "Monkey Trail."

The Spanish RUI (www.riu.com) hotel group plans to build three luxury hotels totaling 2,000 rooms at Playa Matapalo. First up will be the 700-room **Hotel Riu Guanacaste,** Costa Rica's largest hotel to date, slated to open in November 2009 with a casino, spa, and conference center.

The following beaches are listed in north to south order, assuming access via the "Monkey Trail."

PLAYAS POTRERO AND AZÚCAR

The "Monkey Trail" emerges at Playa Potrero, about 16 kilometers southwest of Sardinal and immediately northeast of Playa Flamingo, from which it is separated by Bahía Potrero. The gray-sand beach curls southward for about three kilometers from the rustic and charming fishing hamlet of Potrero and is popular with campers during holidays.

North of Potrero, a dirt road leads to **Playa Penca,** a beautiful beach backed by a protected mangrove estuary—that of the Río Salinas—and rare saltwater forest replete with bird-life, including parrots, roseate spoonbills, and egrets. From Penca, the road snakes north three kilometers to Playa Azúcar (Sugar Beach), a narrow, 400-meter-wide spit of sun-drenched, coral-colored sand that just might have you dreaming of retiring here. There's good snorkeling offshore.

Accommodations

You can camp at **Mayra's Camping and Cabins** (tel. 506/2654-4213, $5 campsites, $20–35 cabins), a friendly beachfront spot with showers, toilets, and a small *soda* where Mayra makes *típico* and seafood dishes.

At **Cabinas Cristina** (tel. 506/2654-4006, www.cabinascristina.com, $50 s/d room, $60 mini-apartment) you have the benefit of a small pool. The six simple, all-wood, air-conditioned *cabinas* are set in shady albeit unkempt gardens and each sleeps four people, with private bathrooms and hot water, plus free Wi-Fi.

The Italian-run **Hotel Isolina** (tel. 506/2654-4333, www.isolinabeach.com, $45–55 s/d room, from $75 villa low season; $60–75 s/d room, from $90 villa high season), one kilometer south of Potrero, has 11 attractive if simple and somewhat dark air-conditioned cabins with cable TVs, and private bathrooms with hot water. It also has three villas and rooms in a twin-story hotel complex, plus a pool and restaurant in lush gardens.

Bahía Esmeralda Hotel and Restaurant (tel. 506/2654-4480, www.hotelbahiaesmeralda .com, $50 s or $60 d rooms, $70–116 apartments low season; $60 s or $70 d rooms, $93–142 apartments high season) is a modern, Italian-run hotel 200 meters on the southern edge of Potrero hamlet. The four simply furnished rooms, four houses, and eight apartments feature red-tile roofs and have all cable TV, lofty hardwood ceilings, double beds and bunks, and modern conveniences. Italian fare is served in an open-sided restaurant, and there's a swimming pool in lush gardens. Horseback tours and bike rental are available, as is a boat for turtle tours and fishing.

Villagio Flor de Pacífico (tel. 506/2654-4664, www.flordepacifico.com), on the "Monkey Trail" 400 meters inland of Potrero village and a 15-minute walk from the beach, is a modern Italian-run resort amid lush expansive gardens. Its 50 modestly furnished one- and two-bedroom villas get hot but have air-conditioning fans, lofty wooden ceilings, and cool tile floors, plus kitchens. Facilities include two pools, tennis, and an Italian restaurant. Call for rates.

The gorgeous **Hotel Bahía del Sol** (tel. 506/2654-4671, www.bahiadelsolhotel.com, $140 s/d standard, $175 s/d deluxe, $220–270 suites low season; $165 s/d standard, $190 s/d deluxe, $250–375 suites high season), at Playa Potrero, is a classy beach resort with colorful decor in its 13 rooms and 15 one- and two-bedroom suites, all with air-conditioning. Romantically lit at night, the resort has a gorgeous walk-in pool with swim-up bar plus handsome thatched open-air restaurant. The same owners operate the equally colorful **Catalinas Beach Suites** (tel. 506/2654-4671, fax 506/2654-5005, www.catalinasbeachsuites.com, $190–290 s/d low season, $240–360 s/d high season), with nicely furnished self-contained suites and a freeform pool.

I also recommend the gracious **Hotel Sugar Beach** (tel. 506/2654-4242, www.sugar -beach.com, $125–155 s/d standard, $155 s/d deluxe, $195–350 suites high season; 20 percent less in low season), offering the privacy of a secluded setting on a beachfront rise amid 10 hectares of lawns and forest full of wildlife. The hotel received an exciting contemporary livery in 2006, when a complete overhaul was completed. Choose from 16 new rooms in eight handsome Spanish colonial-style duplexes, or 10 units connected by stone pathways. Also available are a three-bedroom beach house and an apartment suite. A large open-air restaurant looks over the beach, and there's a small pool, horseback rides, and tours. Costa Rica Outriggers is based here.

New in 2009, the contemporary Mediterranean-themed **Hotel Mediterraneus** (tel. 506/2297-1029, www.hotelmediterraneus.com, rates vary monthly, from $160 s/d) will have 52 deluxe rooms, a spa, and extensive recreational facilities.

Rosewood Hotels & Resorts (www.rosewoodhotels.com) plans to build the superdeluxe resort **Rosewood Costa Carmel** at Playa Zapotal, north of Azúcar, due to open in 2012.

Food

A favorite of locals, **Maxwell's Café** (tel. 506/2645-4319, 8 A.M.–noon and 4 –10 P.M. daily), 300 meters inland of the beach, is an open-air bar and grill serving American fare. However, by far the best place is the open-air beachfront restaurant at **Bahía del Sol** (tel. 506/2654-4671, 6 A.M.–10 P.M. daily, $5–20), specializing in seafood and continental cuisine; it has a "*fiesta tropical*" on Friday night, and karaoke on Saturday.

Super Wendy (tel. 506/2654-4291), on the main road between Potrero and Flamingo, specializes in gourmet foodstuffs.

Information and Services

A **Welcome Center** (tel. 506/2654-5460) offers tourist information in the new Plaza Casa del Sol, to the northwest of the Potrero village soccer field; there's a **police station** on the south side of the soccer field.

PLAYA FLAMINGO

Playa Flamingo, immediately south of Potrero and facing it from the west side of the bay, is named for the two-kilometer-wide scimitar of white sand—one of the most magnificent beaches in Costa Rica—that lines the north end of Bahía Flamingo (there are no flamingos). The area is favored by wealthy Ticos and gringos (North Americans now own most of the land hereabouts), and expensive villas sit atop the headlands north and south of the beach, many with their own little coves as private as one's innermost thoughts.

The marina was closed by the government

Playa Flamingo

for health reasons in 2006. It remained closed in late 2008 but was due to be rebuilt.

Entertainment and Events

The **Monkey Bar** at the Flamingo Marina Resort has a happy hour daily at 5:30 P.M. It has live music on Friday, barbecue on Saturday, ESPN with pizza on Sunday, and Monday night football (in season). The always-lively bar at the **Mariner Inn** (6 A.M.– 10 P.M. daily) features cable TV and has live music at times.

Disco Amberes (tel. 506/2654-4001, 5 P.M.– 2 A.M.), on the hill, has a spacious lounge bar, a lively disco, and a small casino that opens at 8 P.M. Live bands occasionally play starting at 9:30 P.M. Video slots and card tables are offered at **Flamingo Bay Resort** (tel. 506/2654-4444, 7 P.M.–3 A.M.).

Sports and Recreation

Costa Rica Diving (tel./fax 506/2654-4148, www.costarica-diving.com) offer diving to Islas Murciélagos, as does **Grupo Brindisi** (100 meters east of the marina, tel. 506/2654-4946, www.brindisicr.com), which also has kayak-snorkeling trips, ATV tours, and diving.

Billfish Safaris (tel. 506/2654-5244), next to the Mariner Inn, has sportfishing and ATV tours.

EcoTrans (tel. 506/2654-5151, www.ecotrans costarica.com), in Flamingo Marina Resort, offers tours to Palo Verde National Park, Guaitíl, and other destinations.

And **Flamingo Equestrian Center** (tel. 506/8846-7878, http://equestriancostarica .com) offers horse-riding instruction.

Accommodations

There are no budget properties. The least expensive option is the **Mariner Inn** (tel. 506/2654-4081, fax 506/2654-4024, marinerinn@ racsa.co.cr, $35 s/d standard, $48 with a/c and fridge, $70 suite year-round), a 12-room Spanish colonial-style hotel down by the marina. Dark hardwoods fill the air-conditioned rooms that feature color TVs, blue-and-white tile work, and terra-cotta tile floors. A suite has a mini-bar and kitchenette. There's a pool, and the bar gets lively.

The three-story, haphazardly arranged **Flamingo Marina Resort** (tel. 506/2654-4141 or U.S. tel. 800/276-7501, www.flamingo marina.com, $89 s/d room, $139–149 s/d suite, $169–210 apartments low season; $119 s/d room, $169–189 s/d suite, $209–280 apartments high season), on the hill overlooking the marina, has grand views toward Playa Potrero. It offers three types of accommodations in 123 spacious air-conditioned rooms with lively contempo decor. Suites have king-size beds, plus whirlpools on private terraces. And there are larger, beachfront, one- to three-bedroom apartments. The pleasant terrace restaurant opens onto a circular swimming pool with the thatched swim-up Monkey Bar. Tennis, a gift shop, tour office, and full-service dive shop are also offered. Rates include breakfast and tax.

Down by the beach, and a better bargain, is the **Flamingo Beach Resort** (tel. 506/2654-4444, www.resortflamingobeach.com, $118–131 s/d low season, $132–149 s/d high season), a large-scale complex centered on a voluminous pool with a swim-up bar. The 120 spacious air-conditioned rooms and suites in five types have finally been redone in a smart and colorful contemporary mode. All have fans and 29-inch flat-screen TVs plus free Internet access, minibars, and coffeemakers. Suites have kitchenettes and whirlpool tubs. There are three bars, two restaurants, tennis, large gym, Turkish bath, game room, beauty salon, souvenir shop, rental car agency, dive shop, and casino.

For your own luxurious hilltop villa, check into **Casa Bella** (tel. 919/820-6972, www.luxuryflamingovilla.com, $2,850 weekly), with five bedrooms and a pool.

Food

For unpretentious dining I like the thatched, breeze-swept **Soda Restaurante Pleamar** (tel. 506/2654-4521, 7 A.M.–4 P.M. Mon., 7 A.M.–9 P.M. Tues.–Sun., $5–15), with a splendid beachfront site 400 meters east of the Flamingo marina. It serves ceviche, burgers, lobster, and garlic fish, all for less than $10.

My favorite place is **Marie's Restaurant** (tel. 506/2654-4136, 6:30 A.M.–9:30 P.M. daily), now in ritzy new open-air digs under a huge thatched *palenque* in Centro Comercial La Plaza, 50 meters west of the marina. Aged terra-cotta floor tiles add to the ambience. It offers great breakfasts like granola and omelettes. Lunch and dinner brings fish and chips, chicken from the wood oven, rib eye steak ($14), barbecue pork ribs ($12), and a large selection of sandwiches, plus ice cream sundaes, cappuccinos, lattes, mochas, and espressos.

If chic 21st-century styling is your thing, opt for **Angelina's** (tel. 506/2654-4839, no set hours), which opened in November 2008 upstairs in Centro Comercial La Plaza. It offers international fusion dishes, such as yellow-fin tuna poke starter ($7), and oven-roasted chicken topped with orange espresso glaze ($12). I love the decor! Imagine cowhide ceiling lamps, a bar made of a sliced tree trunk, leather sofas, and a slick lounge bar. Confirmation, indeed, that Flamingo now rocks!

Hitching Post Plaza, two kilometers south of Flamingo and mid-way to Brasilito, has three little gems. **Barnie's Smokehouse** (tel. 506/2654-5827, 9 A.M.–6:30 P.M. Tues.–Fri.) serves smoked chicken, ribs, and salads. Next door, **Cecile's** (tel. 506/2654-5449, 7 A.M.–7 P.M. Mon.–Sat.) serves fresh-baked goods, which you can enjoy at the adjoining **Café Crema** coffee shop, which has Wi-Fi.

Supermercado Flamingo is located at Plaza Que Pasa.

Information and Services

There's a **tourist information center** (tel. 506/2654-4021, www.infoflamingo.com) in Centro Comercial La Plaza; plus a bank, clinic, and pharmacy on the hill above the marina. For an **ambulance** call 506/2654-5523; for **police,** call 506/2654-5647.

Centro Panamericano de Idiomas (tel. 506/2654-5002, www.cpi-edu.com), 100 meters east of the marina, offers Spanish language courses.

Getting There

Tralapa buses (tel. 506/2221-7202) depart San José for Playa Portrero via Brasilito and Flamingo from Calles 20, Avenidas 3/5, daily at 8 A.M., 10:30 A.M., and 3 P.M. ($5.25, five hours), returning from Portrero at 2:45 A.M., 9 A.M., and 2 P.M. Buses (tel. 506/2680-0392) depart Santa Cruz for Playas Brasilito, Flamingo, and Potrero nine times daily 4 A.M.–5 P.M. Return buses depart for Santa Cruz 6 A.M.–8 P.M.

Grayline (tel. 506/2220-2126, www.grayline costarica.com) and **Interbus** (tel. 506/2283-5573, www.interbusonline.com) operate shuttles between Flamingo/Tamarindo and

San José ($35) plus key tourist destinations throughout Costa Rica.

To get to Flamingo from Playas Coco, Hermosa, or Panamá, take a bus to Comunidad, where you can catch a southbound bus for Santa Cruz or Nicoya; get off at Belén, and catch a bus for Flamingo.

PLAYA CONCHAL AND BRASILITO

The hamlet of Brasilito, about four kilometers south of Flamingo and three kilometers north of Huacas, draws an incongruous mix of offbeat budget travelers and the packaged all-inclusive resort set, drawn to the massive Paradisus Playa Conchal Beach & Golf Resort, a five-star hotel within the huge **Reserva Conchal** (tel. 506/2654-4000, www.reserva conchal.com) residential community.

The light-gray sand beach at Brasilito melds westward into Playa Conchal, one of Costa Rica's finest beaches. The beach lies in the cusp of a scalloped bay with turquoise waters, a rarity in Costa Rica. The beach is composed, uniquely, of zillions of tiny seashells that move with soft rustling sounds as you walk; the waters are of crystalline quality perfect for snorkeling. It's illegal to remove shells. Please leave them for future generations to enjoy.

Conchal can also be accessed by road from the west via the hamlet of **Matapalo,** three kilometers west of Huacas, where a rough dirt road leads from the northwest corner of the soccer field to the west end of Playa Conchal (4 km). A side road on the Matapalo-Conchal road leads west to **Playa Real,** a stunning little beauty of a beach nestled in a sculpted bay with a tiny tombolo leading to a rocky island. Venerable fishing boats make good resting spots for pelicans.

This region is booming! Roads have been cut to heretofore isolated beaches, such as **Playa Nombre de Jesús,** the setting for several new deluxe hotels in the works.

Sports and Recreation

Costa Rica Temptations (tel. 506/2654-4585, www.costarica4u.com, 8 A.M.–6 P.M. Mon.–Fri. and 8 A.M.–2 P.M. Sat.–Sun.), 100

angler with catch, Playa Nombre de Jesús

© CHRISTOPHER P. BAKER

meters south of the soccer field, offers tours throughout the region.

Santana Tours (tel. 506/2654-4359), opposite Hotel Conchal, offers ATV (all-terrain vehicle) tours, horseback rides, and scooter rental. And **Qcho's Shop** (tel. 506/2654-5704), nearby, specializes in surfing.

There are water sports concessions on Playa Conchal. You can buy day (8 A.M.–5 P.M.) and/or night (6 P.M.–1 A.M.) passes ($65) that permit nonguests to use the Paradisus resort facilities. Its highlight is the **Garra de León Golf Club,** with an 18-hole golf course designed by the king of designers, Robert Trent Jones, Jr.; it is not open to walk-ins, but guests at local hotels can play by reservation.

Accommodations

You can camp under shade trees ($2 pp low season, $3 high season) behind the beach at **Brasilito Lodge** (tel./fax 506/2654-4452, www.brasilito-conchal.com), an otherwise unkempt place that also has seven motley cabins not worth recommending.

The **Cabinas Ojos Azules** (tel./fax 506/2654-4346, www.cabinasojosazules.com, from $10 pp), 100 meters south of the soccer field, has 14 clean and neatly furnished yet basic cabins for up to eight people. Some have hot water. There's a laundry, a small plunge pool, and a *rancho* with hammocks.

The German-run **Hotel Brasilito** (tel. 506/2654-4237, www.brasilito.com, $29–60 s/d low season; $39–70 s/d high season), 50 meters from both the beach and soccer field, is a well-run hotel with 15 simple rooms (they vary greatly; some are air-conditioned) with fans and private baths with hot water, in a daffodil-yellow wooden home adorned with flowerboxes. It has an atmospheric restaurant.

My favorite place here is **Hotel Conchal** (tel. 506/2654-9125, http://conchalcr.com, $65 s, $85 d), 200 meters south of the soccer field. This charming Polynesian-style hotel is run by an English-Danish couple and has nine pretty, whitewashed, tile-floored air-conditioned rooms with wrought-iron beds (some are king-size), ceiling fans, TVs, halogen lighting, and river-stone exteriors. They face a landscaped garden full of bougainvillea. The Robinson Crusoe–style upstairs lounge is a delightful space. A dive school is on-site.

Next door, the new **Cabinas Diversion Tropical** (tel. 506/2654-5519, www.diversion tropical.com, $37 s/d, or $47 with kitchenette) has 12 clean, simply appointed rooms in a two-story unit.

Apartotel & Restaurant Nany (tel. 506/ 2654-4320, www.apartotelnany.com, $60–75 s/d low season, $93–110 s/d high season) has 11 uniquely designed, spacious, modern, air-conditioned two-bedroom "apartments" with kitchenettes and tall half-moon windows, ceiling fans, cable TV, security box, and private baths with hot water. It has an open-air restaurant and a plunge pool.

The U.S.–run **Condor Heights** (tel. 506/2653-8950, www.condorheights.com, $225 low season, $250 high season, three-night minimum), atop the hill 600 meters inland and south of Playa Conchal, rents fully furnished condominiums. The open-terrace dining room—offering spectacular views—is topped by a lofty lounge bar and casino. There's also a TV lounge and small library. A swimming pool with cascade

is set on the lofty sundeck. A new alternative for the self-catering set is **Finca Buena Fuente Hotel** (tel. 506/8359-8183, www.buenafuente hotel.com, $60–150 s/d low season, $20 each additional person), combining traditional farm-style restaurant and bar with huge, modern apartment units furnished in spartan, uninspired fashion. Units differ; some have loft bedrooms. It's one kilometer from the beach.

For a more luxurious experience, check into the **Paradisus Playa Conchal Beach & Golf Resort** (tel. 506/2654-4123, www.solmelia.com, from $378 s/d), spanning 285 hectares and surrounded by rippling fairways. The resort has 308 open-plan junior suites and two master suites in 37 two-story units amid landscaped grounds behind the beach. They are beautiful, with exquisite marble bathrooms, mezzanine bedrooms supported by columns, and lounges with soft-cushioned sofas. The massive free-form swimming pool is a setting for noisy aerobics and games. It has three restaurants, two bars, a disco, a theater with nightly shows, tennis courts, plus the golf course. However, readers have complained that meals are mediocre and outrageously priced.

Playa Real is the setting for the Italian-run **Bahía de Las Piratas Resort** (tel. 506/2653-8951, www.bahiadelospiratas.com). Alas, this complex of 15 Spanish colonial-style condos and villas has deteriorated markedly and can no longer be recommended, despite its lovely location.

In 2007, ground was broken on the **Hyatt Regency Azulera** (www.hyatt.com), a 225-hectare resort with a 214-room hotel, 1,000 private residences, and a Greg Norman–designed golf course. In 2008 it fell afoul of environmental investigators, and at press time its future was uncertain.

Canyon Ranch Costa Rica, a deluxe spa resort, is planned for Playa Nombre de Jesús, with a Gary Player–designed golf course.

Food

Don't leave town without dining at the Hotel Brasilito's breezy, **Outback Jack's Australian Road Kill Grill** (tel. 506/2654-4596, 7 A.M.– 11 P.M. daily), festooned with intriguing miscellany and serving killer breakfasts such as grilled croissants and eggs ranchero ($3). The wide-ranging lunch and dinner menu ranges from ceviche and shrimp on the barbie to lasagna and grilled pork loin. There's a large-screen TV for sports events.

Information and Services

The **police station** (tel. 506/2654-4425) is on the main road, facing the soccer field. The **Miracle Medical Center & Pharmacy** (tel. 506/2654-4996) is nearby, and there's a major medical center (tel. 506/2654-5440) in nearby Huacas.

Café Internet Nany is at Apartotel & Restaurant Nany (tel. 506/2654-4320, www .apartotelnany.com). **Books & More Books** (tel. 506/2653-7373), in Paseo del Mar Commercial Center, three kilometers south of Brasilito, sells guidebooks and novels in English.

Getting There and Around

The Flamingo-bound buses from San José and Santa Cruz stop in Matapalo and Brasilito.

For a taxi call 506/8836-1739. **Adobe Rent-a-Car** (tel. 506/8811-4242, www.adobecar .com) is in Conchal Commercial Center.

Tamarindo and Vicinity

Tamarindo, a former fishing village that has burgeoned into Guanacaste's most developed (some would say overdeveloped) resort, offers prime wildlife viewing, a scintillating beach, surfing action, and a choice of accommodations spanning shoestring to sophisticated.

Recent years have seen a growth in robberies against tourists. Rental car break-ins are common. Drugs and prostitution have also encroached, and hustlers can be a nuisance.

◖ MARINO LAS BAULAS NATIONAL PARK

Costa Rican beaches don't come more beautiful than **Playa Grande,** a seemingly endless curve of sand (varying from coral-white to gray) with water as blue as the summer sky. A beach trail to the north leads along the cape through dry forest and deposits you at **Playa Ventanas,** with tidepools for snorkeling and bathing. Surf pumps ashore at high tide. Surfing expert Mark Kelly rates Playa Grande as "maybe the best overall spot in the country."

The entire shoreline is protected within the 445-hectare Parque Nacional Marino Las Baulas (a.k.a. Playa Grande Marine Turtle National Park), which guards the prime nesting site of the leatherback turtle on the Pacific coast, including 22,000 hectares out to sea. The beach was

incorporated into the national park system in May 1990 after a 15-year battle between developers and conservationists. The park is the result of efforts by Louis Wilson, owner of Hotel Las Tortugas, and his former wife, Marianel Pastor. The government agreed to support the couple's conservation efforts only if they could show that the site was economically viable as a tourist destination. The locals, who formerly harvested the turtles' eggs (as did a cookie company), have taken over all guiding (each guide is certified through an accredited course). However, much of the land backing the beach has recently been developed with condos, homes, and hotels. While MINAE officials contemplate tearing down some of these for violating environmental laws, other officials reportedly have recently granted permission for a Best Western Hotel to be built. And fishing boats continue to trawl illegally and unpoliced within the sanctuary with landlines, which snag turtles!

The beach sweeps south to the mouth of the Río Matapalo, which forms a 400-hectare mangrove estuary. This ecosystem is protected within **Tamarindo National Wildlife Refuge** (Refugio Nacional de Vida Silvestre Tamarindo, tel. 506/2296-7074) and features crocodiles, anteaters, deer, ocelots, and monkeys. Waterbirds and raptors gather, especially

THE LEATHERBACK TURTLE

The leatherback turtle (Dermochelys coriacea) is the world's largest reptile and a true relic from the age of the dinosaurs; fossils date back 100 million years. The average adult weighs about 455 kilograms and is two meters in length, though males have been known to attain a staggering 910 kilograms! It is found in all the world's oceans except the Arctic.

Though it nests on the warm beaches of Costa Rica, the baula (as it is locally known) has evolved as a deep-diving cold water critter; its great, near-cylindrical bulk retains body heat in cold waters (it can maintain a body temperature of 18°C in near-frigid water). The leatherback travels great distances, feeding in the open ocean as far afield as subarctic waters, where its black body helps absorb the sun's warming rays. Like seals, the leatherback has a thick oily layer of fat for insulation. Its preferred food is jellyfish.

The females – which reach reproductive age between 15 and 50 years – prefer to nest on steep beaches that have a deepwater approach, thus avoiding long-distance crawls. Nesting occurs during the middle hours of the night – the coolest hours. Leatherback eggs take longer to hatch – 70 days on average – than those of other sea turtles.

Whereas in other turtle species, the boney exterior carapace is formed by flattened, widened ribs that are fused and covered with corneous tissues resembling the human fingernail, the leatherback has an interior skeleton of narrow ribs linked by tiny bony plates all encased by a thick "shell" of leathery, cartilaginous skin. The leatherback's tapered body is streamlined for hydrodynamic efficiency, with seven longitudinal ridges that act like a boat's keel, and long, powerful flippers for maximum propulsion. Leatherbacks have been shown to dive deeper than 1,300 meters, where their small lungs, flexible frames, squishy bodies, and other specialist adaptations permit the animal to withstand well over 1,500 pounds of pressure per square inch.

The species is close to extinction. Contributions to help save leatherback turtles can be sent marked Programa de Tortugas Marinas to Karen and Scott Eckert, **Hubbs Sea World Research Institute** (2595 Ingraham St., San Diego, CA 92109, U.S. tel. 619/226-3870, www.hswri.org), or to the **Leatherback Trust** (161 Merion Av., Haddonfield, NJ 08033, U.S. tel. 215/895-2627, www.leatherback.org).

in dry season. The refuge's ranger station is about 500 meters upriver from the estuary.

The hamlet of **Comunidad Playa Grande** is on the main approach road, 600 meters inland from the beach. The sprawling woodsy community at the southern half of the beach is called Palm Beach Estates.

There's now guarded parking ($2) at the main beach entrance; elsewhere car break-ins are an everyday occurrence. *Don't leave anything in your vehicle.*

The El Mundo de la Tortuga (World of the Turtle museum) has closed.

Visiting the Turtles of Playa Grande

Turtles call at Playa Grande year-round. The nesting season for the giant leatherback is October–March, when females come ashore every night at high tide. Sometimes as many as 100 turtles might be seen in a single night. (Olive ridley turtles and Pacific green turtles can sometimes also be seen here, May–August.) Each female leatherback will nest as many as 12 times a season, every 10 days or so (usually at night to avoid dehydration). Most turtles prefer the center of the beach, just above the high-tide mark.

The beach is open to visitors by day at no cost, and by permit only with a guide at night in nesting season (6 P.M.–6 A.M., $10 entrance with guide; the fee is payable on *leaving* the beach if turtles have been seen); anyone found on the beach at night without a permit in

© CHRISTOPHER P. BAKER

Marino las Baulas National Park

nesting season faces a $1,000 fine (second offense; first offenders are escorted off the beach). Guides from the local community roam the beach and lead groups to nesting turtles; other guides spot for turtles and call in the location via walkie-talkies. Visitors are not allowed to walk the beach after dusk unescorted. Groups cannot exceed 15 people, and only 60 people are allowed onto the beach at night at each of two entry points (four groups per gate, with a maximum of eight groups nightly): one where the road meets the beach by the Hotel Las Tortugas, and the second at the southern end, by Villas Baulas. *Reservations are mandatory,* although entry without a reservation is possible if there's space in a group (don't count on it, as demand usually exceeds supply). You can make reservations up to eight days in advance, or 8 A.M.–5 P.M. for a same-day visit. At certain times the waiting time can be two hours before you are permitted onto the beach; each night differs.

Resist the temptation to follow the example of the many thoughtless visitors who get too close to the turtles, try to touch them,

ride their backs, or otherwise display a lack of common sense and respect. Flashlights and camera flashes are *not* permitted (professional photographers can apply in advance for permission to use a flash). And watch your step. Newborn turtles are difficult to see at night as they scurry down to the sea. Many are inadvertently crushed by tourists' feet.

The park headquarters (Centro Operaciones Parque Nacional Marina las Baulas, tel./fax 506/2653-0470) is 100 meters east of Hotel Las Tortugas. It features an auditorium on turtle ecology. *Viewing the film is obligatory for all people intending to witness the turtles nesting.*

Sports and Recreation

Hotels and tour companies in the area offer turtle-watching tours (about $25) and a "Jungle Boat Safari," aboard a 20-passenger pontoon boat that takes you into the mangrove-rich Tamarindo Wildlife Refuge ($30).

Hotel Las Tortugas (tel. 506/2653-0423, www.lastortugashotel.com) rents surfboards ($15–35) and boogie boards ($10 per day) and has canoe tours of the estuary ($30 solo, $55

© CHRISTOPHER P. BAKER

Playa Grande Surf Camp

guided). **Pura Vida Café** (tel. 506/2653-0835) offers surf lessons ($50), as does **Frijoles Locos** (tel. 506/2652-9235, www.frijoleslocos.com), at the entrance to Playa Grande; it's the best stocked surf store around. Next door, **El Frijol Feliz Day Spa** (tel. 506/2652-9236) can soothe weary muscles with a relaxing massage.

The **Hotel Bula Bula Beach Club** (tel. 506/2653-0975 or U.S. tel. 877/658-2880, www.hotelbulabula.com) at the south end of the beach, has funball, volleyball, ocean kayaks, boogie boards, and *boules*.

Accommodations

Camping is not allowed on the beach. You can camp at **Centro Vacacional Playa Grande** (tel./fax 506/2653-0834, $5 pp) at Comunidad Playa Grande; it has showers and toilets. It also has 12 two-bedroom *cabinas* with private bathrooms with cold water only; eight have kitchenettes ($15 pp fan, $20 pp a/c). There's a restaurant, pool, and free laundry.

For backpackers, I recommend **Playa Grande Surf Camp** (tel. 506/2653-1074, www.playagrandesurfcamp.com, $15 pp dorm, $25 pp cabins). It has three small but delightful, air-conditioned, wood-and-thatch cabins on stilts, plus two A-frames, including a dorm with screened windows. The courtyard has a pool and thatched shade areas with hammocks, plus there's Wi-Fi, board rental, and surf lessons.

The **Playa Grande Inn** (tel./fax 506/2653-0719, www.playagrandeinn.com, $50 s/d room, $75 suite), a handsome surf camp with eight impeccably clean, simply appointed rooms in an all-wood two-story structure. There's a pool, whirlpool tub, and a lively bar. You can also rent an apartment.

There were two striking newcomers in 2008. First is the Italian-run **Sol y Luna Lodge** (tel. 506/8893-0198, www.solylunalodge.net, $30–40 pp), one kilometer inland of the beach. This lovely place has eight tree-shaded thatched cabins (for four or six people) with cable TVs, Indonesian batiks, ceiling fans, mosquito nets, verandas, and nice modern bathrooms with whirlpool tubs. A rustic restaurant was being added beside the landscaped pool with rockwall hot tub and water cascade. Two smaller cabins are air-conditioned and have king-size beds. It has Wi-Fi.

And the **Playa Grande Surf Hotel** (tel. 506/2653-2656, www.playagrandesurfhotel.net, $75 standard, $95 deluxe, $175 suite low season, $125 standard, $150 deluxe, $275 suite high season) belies its name. This modern, two-story, Spanish colonial-style hotel is the most stylish around, with a hip contemporary aesthetic to its rooms and suites, all with flat-screen TVs, Wi-Fi, and air-conditioning. A sushi restaurant was to open in 2009.

Another excellent bet is the ecologically sound **Hotel Las Tortugas** (tel. 506/2653-0423, www.lastortugashotel.com, $35 s/d economy, $50–60 s/d standard, $85 suite low season; $50 economy, $80 standard, $120 suite high season), a comfortable ecolodge. The 12 rooms vary markedly, though all have air-conditioning, pewter-colored stone floors, orthopedic mattresses, cable TV, Wi-Fi, and private baths with hot water. A new suite and some standard rooms have lovely patios and hammocks. The hotel has a turtle-shaped swimming pool with sundeck, plus a large whirlpool tub and a quiet palm-shaded corner with hammocks. (Since newborn turtles are attracted to light and adults can be disoriented by it, there are no ocean views to the south, where the nesting beach is.) The restaurant is a highlight, with an outdoor patio and great food. The hotel rents surfboards and canoes for trips into the estuary ($55 half day) and has horseback riding ($40) and a mangrove boat tour ($25). Louis, the delightful owner, has added eight "student" rooms with bunk beds and shared hot-water shower facilities ($15 s, $20 d).

I like the aesthetic at the **RipJack Inn** (tel. 506/2653-0480, www.ripjackinn.com, $60 s/d standard, $80 s/d *cabina* low season, $80/100 high season), with eight simply appointed rooms graced by Guatemalan fabrics. The open-air restaurant, Upstairs @ the RipJack, serves nouvelle Costa Rican fare and has ocean views. Yoga fans will appreciate the yoga studio.

I adore the █ **Hotel Bula Bula** (tel. 506/2653-0975 or U.S. tel. 877/658-2880, www.hotelbulabula.com, $95 s/d low season, $120 s/d high season), in lush gardens adjoining the mangrove estuary, two kilometers south of Las Tortugas. This attractive place is in the hands of two vivacious U.S. entrepreneurs, one a professional restaurateur. The 10 air-conditioned rooms are fabulous, with rich color schemes, king-size beds with orthopedic mattresses, batik wall hangings, plus fans, fresh-cut flower arrangements, batik sarongs for use by the pool, and a shady balcony. The rooms surround a pool in a landscaped garden. It has a stage for live music. The excellent restaurant and bar (with Wi-Fi and loaner laptops) are popular with locals. A free water-taxi to Tamarindo is available.

Playa Grande is a great place to kick back in your own home. The French-run **Hotel Manglar** (tel. 506/2653-0952, www.hotel-manglar.com) has 10 apartments that surround a lovely amoeba-shaped pool. However, in spring 2008, several private homes, most of which double as vacation rentals, were to be torn down as they lie within the 50-meter zone.

For greater intimacy, and great for families, try **Casa Verde** (tel. 506/2653-0481, casaverdecr@yahoo.com, $135 room, or $285 entire house), a lovely modern home with pool. Three simply appointed, air-conditioned rooms with cable TV have glass sliding doors opening to broad eaves shading terra-cotta patios. One room has a king-size bed and kitchen.

Food

You don't have to leave the beach to eat. Just pop up to **Taco Star** (9 A.M.–sunset), a grill at the park entrance. Jay sells burgers and more. Here, too, the **Hotel Las Tortugas** has an airy restaurant (7:30 A.M.–9:30 P.M. daily) serving an eclectic menu; leave room for the apple pie and ice cream.

Inland, **Centro Vacacional Playa Grande** has an inexpensive *soda* selling *típico* dishes.

For true gourmet fare, head to the elegant █ **Great Waltinis** (5:30–8:30 P.M. Tues.–Thurs., 5:30–9 P.M. Fri.–Sat.) restaurant at Hotel Bula Bula. It serves international cuisine, including quesadillas, chicken wings, shrimp and crab cakes, plus such superbly executed dishes as duckling with mango chutney ($14), filet mignon ($16), and filet of ahi tuna sautéed with white wine and garlic butter ($12). Leave room for the "Siberia" chocolate drink-dessert. Avoid the superb killer martinis if you're driving!

You can stock up at **Super Pura Vida,** in Comunidad Playa Grande, or at **Super Malinche** (tel. 506/2653-0236), which has a thatched seafood restaurant attached.

Getting There

From Flamingo, road access is via Matapalo, six kilometers east of Playa Grande (turn left at the soccer field in Matapolo). A rough dirt road also links Tamarindo and Playa Grande via Villareal. The Flamingo-bound buses from San José and Santa Cruz stop in Matapalo, where you can catch a taxi or the bus that departs Santa Cruz at 6 A.M. and 1 P.M.; the return bus departs Playa Grande at 7:15 A.M. and 3:15 P.M.

Tamarindo Shuttle (tel. 506/2653-2727) charges $24 for "door-to-door" service from Liberia airport; a taxi will cost about $80.

The **Asociación de Guías Locales** (tel. 506/2653-1687, 7 A.M.–4 P.M.) offers water-taxi between Tamarindo and a dock on the estuary near the Hotel Bula Bula every two hours ($3).

TAMARINDO

Playa Tamarindo, eight kilometers south of Huacas, is Nicoya's most developed beach resort and is especially popular with backpacking surfers. The gray-sand beach is about two kilometers wide, and very deep when the tide goes out—perfect for strolling and watching pelicans dive for fish. It has rocky outcrops, good for tidepooling. There's a smaller beach south of the main beach, with tidepools and relatively fewer people. Riptides are common, so ask locals in the know for the safest places to swim. The Río Matapalo washes onto the beach at its northern end, giving direct access to the Tamarindo Wildlife Refuge via the Estero Palo Seco; a boatman will ferry you for $0.50. You can also wade across at low tide, although crocodiles are sometimes present, as they are in the mangroves at the eastern end of Playa Tamarindo.

To the south, separated by a headland from Playa Tamarindo, is the rapidly evolving, more upscale **Playa Langosta,** a beautiful white-sand beach that stretches beyond the wide estuary of the Río Tamarindo for several kilometers.

Tamarindo has changed beyond recognition in the past decade, metamorphosing from a sleepy surfers' hangout to a full-blown resort, with uncontrolled development in the past few years. High-rise condominiums have arrived, as have shopping malls. But most roads remain unpaved—dusty as hell in dry season and deplorably potholed with vast pools of mud in wet season. Fecal contamination of the ocean has reached dangerous levels. And prostitutes, drug dealers, and a serious crime wave are now part of the scene.

Entertainment and Events

Costa Rica's annual **International Music Festival** is hosted in July and August at Hotel Cala Luna and Villa Alegre B&B.

The **Monkey Bar,** at Tamarindo Vista Villas (tel. 506/2653-0114), has Monday night football, with free shots at touchdowns; Wednesday is ladies' night, with free cocktails for the gals; Thursday is all-you-can-eat pasta; on Friday, the Monkey Bar is still popular for tequila shooters night.

At last visit the no-frills open-air **Pacifico Bar** (formerly Mambo) in the village center was a happening spot on Sunday for reggae night; it has a pool table and music but has had a history of drawing hookers, druggies, and a raffish crowd. **Babylon,** an outdoor bar, hops on Thursday (reggae night), although reportedly it can get violent after midnight! Less salacious, the **Rey Sol Disco Bar** (tel. 506/8301-3609, Fri.–Tues.) is the happening dance scene for the surf crowd; it recently added a huge video screen; Monday is ladies' night, Wednesday is martini night, and hip-hop fans should head there on Fridays. Across the street, the **Voodoo Lounge** (tel. 506/2653-0100, www.elvoodoo.com, 6 P.M.–1 A.M.) has Brazilian

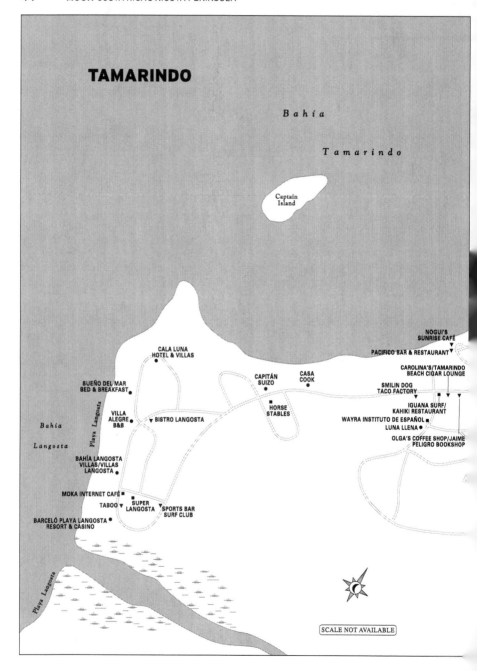

TAMARINDO

Bahía

Tamarindo

Captain
Island

NOGUI'S
SUNRISE CAFÉ

PACIFICO BAR & RESTAURANT

CALA LUNA
HOTEL & VILLAS

CAROLINA'S/TAMARINDO
BEACH CIGAR LOUNGE

CASA
COOK

CAPITÁN
SUIZO

SMILIN DOG
TACO FACTORY

SUEÑO DEL MAR
BED & BREAKFAST

IGUANA SURF/
KAHIKI RESTAURANT

HORSE
STABLES

WAYRA INSTITUTO DE ESPAÑOL

VILLA
ALEGRE
B&B

BISTRO LANGOSTA

LUNA LLENA

Bahía

OLGA'S COFFEE SHOP/JAIME
PELIGRO BOOKSHOP

Langosta

BAHÍA LANGOSTA
VILLAS/VILLAS
LANGOSTA

MOKA INTERNET CAFÉ

TABOO

SUPER
LANGOSTA

SPORTS BAR
SURF CLUB

BARCELÓ PLAYA LANGOSTA
RESORT & CASINO

Playa Langosta

Playa Langosta

SCALE NOT AVAILABLE

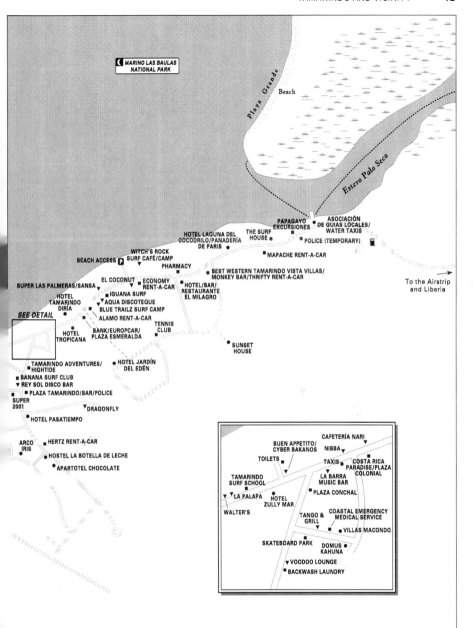

MARINO LAS BAULAS
NATIONAL PARK

Playa Grande

Beach

Estero Palo Seco

To the Airstrip
and Liberia

PAPAGAYO
EXCURSIONES

ASOCIACIÓN
DE GUIAS LOCALES/
WATER TAXIS

THE SURF
HOUSE

POLICE (TEMPORARY)

HOTEL LAGUNA DEL
COCODRILO/PANADERÍA
DE PARIS

MAPACHE RENT-A-CAR

WITCH'S ROCK
SURF CAFÉ/CAMP

BEACH ACCESS

PHARMACY

BEST WESTERN TAMARINDO VISTA VILLAS/
MONKEY BAR/THRIFTY RENT-A-CAR

SUPER LAS PALMERAS/SANSA

EL COCONUT

ECONOMY
RENT-A-CAR

HOTEL/BAR/
RESTAURANTE
EL MILAGRO

HOTEL
TAMARINDO
DIRÍA

IGUANA SURF

AQUA DISCOTEQUE

BLUE TRAILZ SURF CAMP

ALAMO RENT-A-CAR

SEE DETAIL

TENNIS
CLUB

HOTEL
TROPICANA

BANK/EUROPCAR/
PLAZA ESMERALDA

SUNSET
HOUSE

TAMARINDO ADVENTURES/
HIGHTIDE

HOTEL JARDÍN
DEL EDÉN

BANANA SURF CLUB

REY SOL DISCO BAR

PLAZA TAMARINDO/BAR/POLICE

SUPER
2001

DRAGONFLY

HOTEL PASATIEMPO

ARCO
IRIS

HERTZ RENT-A-CAR

HOSTEL LA BOTELLA DE LECHE

APARTOTEL CHOCOLATE

CAFETERÍA NARI

BUEN APPETITO/
CYBER BAKANOS

NIBBA

TOILETS

TAXIS

COSTA RICA
PARADISE/PLAZA
COLONIAL

TAMARINDO
SURF SCHOOL

LA BARRA
MUSIC BAR

LA PALAPA

HOTEL
ZULLY MAR

PLAZA CONCHAL

WALTER'S

TANGO &
GRILL

COASTAL EMERGENCY
MEDICAL SERVICE

VILLAS MACONDO

SKATEBOARD PARK

DOMUS
KAHUNA

VOODOO LOUNGE

BACKWASH LAUNDRY

© AVALON TRAVEL

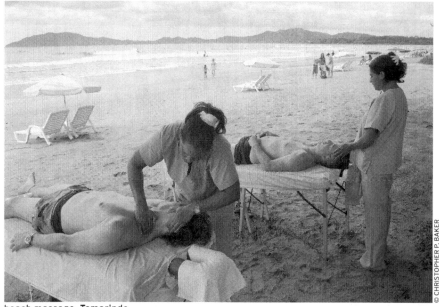

beach massage, Tamarindo

© CHRISTOPHER P. BAKER

acoustic and *carnavale* nights on Monday and Wednesday, respectively. And if you expect the **Copacabana Beach Bar** to have live Brazilian music, you won't be disappointed; go at sunset on Wednesday and Sunday. Meanwhile, **La Barra Music Bar** (tel. 506/2653-0342) hits the groove with Latin Night on Wednesday, and reggae and hip-hop on Saturday.

I expect **Bar 1** (tel. 506/2653-2586, www.bar1tamarindo.com, 6 P.M.–2 A.M.), which opened in November 2008 upstairs in Plaza Tamarindo, to rocket to popularity among martini-sipping city-slickers. Open-air, it has hip black-and-white New York styling. DJs spin on weekends, it shows movies on Tuesday, and it has ladies' night on Thursday. It was adding a sushi restaurant.

And the opening of **Aqua Discoteque** (tel. 506/2653-2782. 10 P.M.–2:30 A.M.) raised the bar with its sexy styling; Monday is ladies' night, with free drinks.

The best sports bar is **Sports Bar Surf Club,** in Playa Langosta, with several pool tables and a classy ambience.

There are **casinos** at the Barceló Playa Langosta (8 P.M.–3 A.M.) and Tamarindo Diría, in Plaza Colonial (6–11 P.M.).

You can surprise your significant other for his or her birthday by hiring any of several Nicaraguan mariachi trios that solicit customers on the beach and main boulevard.

Sports and Recreation

Tamarindo Adventures (tel. 506/2653-0108, www.tamarindoadventuras.com) specializes in ATV tours and kayaking.

Blue Dolphin Sailing (tel. 506/2653-0446, www.sailbluedolphin.com) offers day and sunset cruises, plus snorkeling aboard a 12-meter catamaran, as do **Mandingo Sailing** (tel. 506/2653-2323, www.tamarindosailing.com) and **Seabird Sailing** (tel. 506/8381-1060, www.seabirdsailng.com).

Fishing outfitters include **Tamarindo Sportfishing** (tel. 506/2653-0090, www.tamarindosportfishing.com) and **Papagayo Excursions** (tel. 506/2653-0227, www.papagayoexcursions.com), which also has ATV tours, horseback trips, kayak trips, windsurfing and scuba diving, plus surf tours.

A dozen or so other outlets cater to surfers. **Blue Trailz** (tel. 506/2653-1705, www .bluetrailz.com) is considered the best. **Iguana Surf** (tel. 506/2653-0148, www.iguana surf.net) rents surfboards, offers surf-taxi service to out-of-the-way surfing spots, and has surf lessons, as does **Witch's Rock Surf Camp** (tel. 506/2653-1262, www.witchsrocksurfcamp .com), which also offers weeklong and nine-day surf packages.

For diving, contact **Agua Rica Diving Center** (tel. 506/2653-0094, www.aguarica.net), which has dives and snorkeling from $50.

You can rent horses ($10 per hour) at Hotel Capitán Suizo, which offers guided rides, as does **Painted Pony Guest Ranch** (tel. 506/2653-8041, www.paintedponyguest ranch.com), at Portegolpe.

Off Road Adventures (tel. 506/2653-1968, www.offroadcostarica.com) offers day trips in open-air Toyota four-wheel-drive vehicles.

Tennis buffs can get in the swing at the **Tamarindo Tennis Club** (tel. 506/2653-0898, www.tamarindotennisclub.com, 7:30 A.M.–9 P.M. daily), which has lessons and clinics.

There's even a **skateboard park** now, opposite Villas Macondo.

Shopping

There's no shortage of boutiques and roadside stalls selling quality souvenirs. For something unique, check out **Tamarindo Beach Cigar Lounge** (tel. 506/2653-0862), where Nicaraguan rollers produce superb-quality cigars, including a robust "Espresso" brand, made of Cuban leaves aged with espresso beans, and "La Flor de Palmar," sold in a box in the form of a traditional Costa Rican ox-cart ($178 for 25 Churchills). It has a smoking lounge.

Accommodations

Tamarindo has dozens of options; those listed here are recommended in their price bracket. There are many more hotels than can be listed here.

UNDER $25

Backpackers are spoiled for choice. My favorite place is ◖ **Hostel La Botella de Leche** (tel. 506/2653-2061, www.labotelladeleche.com, $10 pp dorm, $20 s, $35 d private room low season, $12 pp dorm, $30 s, $36 d high season), one of the most popular surfers' and backpackers' spots in the country. It is run to high standards by a delightful Argentinian woman, Mariana "Mama" Nogaro; her son Wences offers surfing tuition. The place (now in its third location) is painted like a Holstein cow! It has a laundry, a delightful lounge, a large common kitchen, plus surf rental, Internet and Wi-Fi, and lockers. It has three dorms, plus six private rooms for up to four people.

Another great bet is the beachfront **Witch's Rock Surf Camp** (tel. 506/2653-1262, www .witchsrocksurfcamp.com, from $1,100 for seven days), a lively place with great ambience. It has clean, colorful, nicely appointed oceanfront rooms, plus a swimming pool, game rooms, thatched restaurant, lockers, a surf shop, and surfing lessons. It specializes in one-week surf packages.

The equally impressive **Blue Trailz Surf Camp** (tel. 506/2653-1705, www.bluetrailz .com) and **Tamarindo Backpackers** (tel. 506/2653-2753, www.tamarindobackpackers .com) compete.

$25-50

Readers rave about **Villas Macondo** (tel. 506/2653-0812, www.villasmacondo.com, $25 s or $30 d with fan, $45 s or $50 d with a/c, $70–105 apartment low season; $35 s or $40 d with fan, $55 s or $65 d with a/c, $105–140 apartment high season), run by a German couple. This delightful spot has five colorful albeit simply appointed double rooms with ceiling fans. Four larger rooms have air-conditioning. Or, choose spacious, fully equipped, two-story one- or two-bedroom apartments. There's a community kitchen, and you can cool off in a kidney-shaped pool.

$50-100

French-run **La Laguna del Cocodrilo Hotel** (tel.

506/2653-0255, www.lalagunadelcocodrilo
.com, $45–90 s/d low season, $60–115 s/d
high season) has a unique location: the natural back garden merges into the adjacent
lagoon with crocodiles. The hotel remodeled and went more upscale in 2008 and has
added a restaurant and lounge. It has 12 air-
conditioned rooms and two ocean-view suites,
all with cable TV and minimalist but charming decor including terra-cotta tile floors,
batik wall hangings, ceiling fans, and beautiful glazed bathrooms with hot water. Some
rooms have stone terraces facing the beach.
It has a bakery.

In the center, **Hotel Zully Mar** (tel. 506/
2653-0140, http://zullymar.com, $41 s or $46
d low season, $56 s or $61 d high season) has
raised itself from shoestring status and is now
a well-run property with 27 clean rooms (eight
with a/c, refrigerator, and safe) with private
baths, though most still have cold water. The
old wing is still popular with backpackers (despite being overpriced), though a newer wing
has metamorphosed Zully Mar into a simple
albeit stylish hotel with a pool.

The attractive **Hotel/Bar/Restaurante El
Milagro** (tel. 506/2653-0043, www.elmilagro
.com, $67 s or $72 d low season, $87 s or $92 d
high season) has charm. The 32 modern conical *cabinas*—set in soothing, breezy, landscaped
grounds with a swimming pool—have air-
conditioning and private baths with hot water.
A restaurant serves seafood under the watch-
ful guidance of European management. There's
also a kids' pool. Rates include breakfast.

Domus Kahuna (tel. 506/2653-0648,
www.domuskahuna.com, $50 s or $60 d
rooms, $75 one-bedroom apartments, $115
two-bedroom apartments low season; $60 s,
$75 d room, $115 one-bedroom apartments,
$155 two-bedroom apartments high season)
has three simply furnished one-bedroom and
three two-bedroom apartments in a landscaped
garden. Rough-hewn timbers add a nice note to
the earth-tone structures, with classic Central
American architectural hints. It has free Wi-Fi
and a swimming pool.

I like the new beachfront **La Palapa** (tel.

506/2653-0362, www.lapalapatamarindo.com,
$65 s, $75 d), tucked up to the beach in the
village center. Its compact loft bedrooms are
endearingly furnished and have cable TVs,
minibars, and safes. It has an enviable location,
and a pleasing restaurant with bar. Nice!

The exquisite, Italian-run, canary-yel-
low **Luna Llena** (tel. 506/2653-0082,
www.hotellunallena.com, $75 s/d stan-
dard, $89 bungalows low season; $90 standard, $109 bungalows high season) has
air-conditioned rooms and bungalows around
an alluring swimming pool with swim-up bar
and a raised wooden sundeck with a whirlpool tub. Stone pathways connect sponge-
washed conical bungalows done up in lively
Caribbean colors and tasteful decor, including
terra-cotta floors; a spiral staircase leads to a
loft bedroom, and the semicircular bathrooms
are marvelous. There's a small restaurant and
a laundry. Rates include tax and breakfast (the
seventh day is free).

Past guests who remember the old Cabinas
Arco Iris won't recognize the new **【 Hotel
Arco Iris** (tel. 506/2653-0330, www.hotel
arcoiris.com, $79 s/d bungalows, $89 s/d deluxe rooms low season; $89 bungalows, $99 deluxe rooms high season) under its new owner.
The two highlights are the gorgeous wood-
and-stone pool deck with lounge chairs, pool,
and the superb Seasons Restaurant. Black stone
pathways link the five bungalows and four upstairs deluxe rooms in sepia-toned units with
timber supports. The lovely yet simple aesthetic combines chocolates and creams, and
all rooms have TV, refrigerator, and gorgeous
contemporary bathrooms with slate walls and
stylish fixtures.

$100-200

Down by the shores, **Hotel Tamarindo Diría**
(tel. 506/2653-0031, www.tamarindodiria
.com, $182–230 year-round) ranks in the top
tier with its quasi-Balinese motif and rich
color scheme, although locals complain that it
dumps waste matter directly into the sea. The
lobby, boasting Guanacastecan pieces and elegant rolled-arm chaise lounges, opens to an

exquisite horizon pool with fountains, with lawns and ocean beyond. It has 113 pleasantly furnished air-conditioned rooms (including 47 deluxe and 28 premium) with terra-cotta tile floors. Some have a whirlpool tub, and many are wheelchair accessible. A large and airy restaurant with a beautiful hardwood ceiling opens onto an expansive bar and outside cocktail terrace. It has a kids' pool, tennis courts, a small casino, golf driving range, and a boutique, plus sportfishing and tours.

The **Hotel Pasatiempo** (tel. 506/2653-0096, www.hotelpasatiempo.com, $89 s/d standard $109 deluxe, $119 suites low season; $109 s/d standard $119 deluxe, $139 suites high season) has 11 attractive, spacious, well-lit, thatched, air-conditioned cabins around a pool in pretty grounds full of bougainvillea, bananas, and palms. Note the beautiful hand-carved doors and hand-painted murals in each room. It has a book exchange, table games, and snorkeling gear. The Yucca Bar hosts live music.

The overpriced, hillside, all-suite **Tamarindo Vista Villas** (tel. 506/653-0114, fax 506/653-0115, www.tamarindovistavillas.com, $144–194 s/d low season, $159–209 s/d high season) offers 32 handsomely appointed, oceanview, air-conditioned one- to three-bedroom suites with full kitchens and spacious verandas. The property has a swimming pool with waterfall, swim-up bar, open-air poolside restaurant, and disco.

Wow! That was my first reaction to **15 Love Contemporary Bed & Breakfast** (tel. 506/2653-0898, www.15lovebedandbreakfast .com, $95 s/d room, $115 suite low season; $125 room, $155 suite high season), at the Tamarindo Tennis Club. Tucked in a courtyard with plunge pool, wooden deck, and sexily sinuous bar, this hip minimalist inspiration has just three rooms and a suite, each with lovely, clean, crisp, colorful, contemporary decor and orthopedic king-size beds, plus flat-screen TV and Wi-Fi. Stylish to the max! You can rent the entire place.

City-style sophistication is also a hallmark at **Hotel Jardín del Edén** (tel. 506/2653-0137, www.jardindeleden.com, $110–150 s/d rooms, $190 suite, $140–170 apartment), on a bluff overlooking Tamarindo. Truly a hillside "garden of Eden," it earns laurels for the chic and amorous tenor of its 34 rooms and two villas with gracious contemporary flair, and spacious terrace-porches offering ocean views. Rooms are themed in regional styles: Japan, Tunisia, Mexico. A stunning pool with swim-up bar, whirlpool tub, and a large sundeck with shady *ranchitos* are set in lush gardens floodlit at night in a quasi-*son et lumière*. The restaurant is one of the best in town. Rates include buffet breakfast.

Not quite as classy, but still a great bet, is the colorful **Cala Luna Hotel and Villas** (tel. 506/2653-0214 or 800/503-5202, www.cala luna.com, $170 s/d room, $345–465 villa low season; $205 s/d room, $410–520 villa high season), at Playa Langosta. Spanish tile and rough-hewn timbers add to the cozy New Mexico–Central American style. The 20 hotel rooms, 16 garden villas, and five master villas surround a pool in a small landscaped garden. King-size beds, cable TVs, and CD players are standard, and each villa has its own pool. There's a boutique and tour desk, pool bar, plus an evocative candlelit restaurant. Tours, horseback rides, and fishing trips are offered.

I love the 🄲 **Sueño del Mar Bed and Breakfast** (tel. 506/2653-0284, www.sueno -del-mar.com, $150–195 low season, $195–240 high season), a truly exquisite Spanish colonial house with four rooms cascading down a shaded alcove to a small landscaped garden that opens onto the beach. Each is cool and shaded, with rough-hewn timbers, white-washed stone walls, terra-cotta tile floors, security boxes, screened arched windows with shutters, and tasteful fabrics. Most have exquisite rainforest showers. The huge upstairs suite is a true gem, with all-around screened windows, mosquito net on the four-poster bed made of logs, and a Goldilocks'-cottage feel to the bathroom with rainforest shower with gorgeous tilework. It also has a *casita* for four people. A small landscaped pool and wooden sundeck has been added, along with thatched shade area with hammock, perfect for enjoying cocktails and *bocas*. Complimentary snorkel gear, boogie boards, and bikes are available.

I also love **Villa Alegre** (tel. 506/2653-0270, www.villaalegrecostarica.com, $150–195 low season, $170–230 high season), a contemporary beachfront bed-and-breakfast run by gracious hosts Barry and Suzye Lawson from California, who specialize in wedding and honeymoon packages. The main house has lofty ceilings, tile floors, lots of hardwood hints, a magnificent lounge with library, and four air-conditioned bedrooms with French doors opening onto a private patio. Two *casitas*—one sleeping four people—each have a living room, bedroom, and small but fully equipped kitchen. The rooms are individually decorated with the globetrotting couple's collection of art, rugs, and miscellany. The Mexico and Russia rooms are wheelchair-accessible. A vast veranda overlooks a swimming pool, with a thatched bar serving *bocas*. Rates include breakfast.

If large-scale resorts are your thing, the handsome **Barceló Playa Langosta Resort & Casino** (tel. 506/2653-0363, www.barcelo.com, from $95 per person low season, from $130 high season), is Tamarindo's first mega-resort. It sits above the river estuary. It has 240 rooms in three categories in nine two- and three-story blocks arrayed around a freeform pool, with a whirlpool for 30, set in lush landscaped grounds. It has a casino, boutique, tour desk, and tours. Rates include tax.

Seeking a self-catering rental? One of my favorites is **Casa Cook** (tel. 506/2653-0125, http://casacook.net, $150–250), about one kilometer west of town, with three one-bedroom *casitas* with a pool and patio. Other choices include two large bedrooms with private baths in the main house and an apartment added in 2007. Alternately, try **The Surf House** (tel. 506/2255-0448, www.thesurfhouse.com, from $140 per night) or look to **Vacation Rentals of Tamarindo** (www.vacationrentalsoftamaraindo.com).

OVER $200

My preferred place to rest my head is the Swiss-run ◖ **Capitán Suizo** (tel. 506/2653-0075, www.hotelcapitansuizo.com, $130–150 s/d rooms, $180–220 bungalow, $300–375 suite low season; $190–210 s/d rooms, $250–290 bungalow, $365–525 suite high season), a deserving member of the Small Distinctive Hotels of Costa Rica. Beach-loving cognoscenti will appreciate the resort's casual sophistication. Even the local howler monkeys have decided this is the place to be! Pathways coil sinuously through a botanical *Fantasia* to a wide sundeck and large amoeba-shaped pool with a faux beach shelving gently into the water. The lovely 22 rooms and eight bungalows (some lack air-conditioning) have natural gray-stone floors and deep-red hardwoods, halogen lamps, and soft-lit lanterns for a more romantic note. Spacious bungalows have mezzanine bedrooms with king-size bed and huge bathrooms with "rainforest" showers and whirlpool tubs. The wood-paneled Honeymoon Suite has a king-size bed in its own loft. The bar and restaurant are among Tamarindo's finest. Capitán Suizo has its own horse stable ($20 first hour, $10 each extra hour), plus kayaks, boogie boards, and a game room.

Yoga anyone? **Panacea de la Montaña** (tel. 506/2653-8515, www.panaceacr.com, $160 s or $240 d low season, $188 s or $260 d high season, including all meals) is a holistic yoga and wellness retreat in the mountains outside Tamarindo, with delightful Tuscan-style cabins and gourmet fare.

Alternately, the supremely deluxe ◖ **Los Altos de Eros** (tel. 560/8850-4222, www.losaltosdeeros.com, $395–495 s/d) graces an 11-hectare estate outside town. This Tuscan-style villa boasts six gorgeous rooms (four poolside), including a two-bedroom suite; all are done up in pure white and are exquisitely romantic. Dinners are served twice weekly. The inn specializes in yoga in a thatched ashram, plus health and beauty treatments in a full-service spa.

Food

Tamarindo is blessed with some of the most creative restaurateurs in the country, and the scene is ever-changing.

The French **Panadería La Laguna del Cocodrilo** (tel. 506/2653-0255, 6 A.M.–7 P.M. daily) offers an all-you-can-eat buffet breakfast in the garden ($5). It also sells delicious croissants, chocolate èclairs, fruit tarts, baguettes, and bread, plus enchiladas and *empanadas* at lunch. For hearty gringo breakfasts, you can't beat the beachfront **Nogui Bar/ Sunrise Café** (tel. 506/2653-0029, 6 A.M.–9:30 P.M. daily).

The **Smilin' Dog Taco Factory** (tel. 506/2653-0658, 11 A.M.–10 P.M. Mon.–Sat.) sells tacos ($1.75), burritos ($3), veggie burritos, quesadillas, and soft drinks (no alcohol). Nearby, Iguana Surf's **Kahiki Restaurant** (tel. 506/2653-3816, 11 A.M.–2 P.M. and 5–10 P.M. Wed.–Mon.) has a great setting under thatch; it makes great burgers ($7) and offers Asian fusion cuisine, such as coconut ceviche ($5) and oven-roasted, herb-rubbed pork tenderloin ($12).

For a cool, unpretentious open-air beach option, try **Nibba** (tel. 506/2654-0447, 7:30 A.M.–10:30 P.M. daily), with an eclectic menu ranging from salads and seafood to pizza and pastas.

The hip **El Jardín del Edén** (noon–10 P.M. daily, lunch $6–13, dinner $15–60), at the hotel of that name, serves fusion dishes such as jumbo shrimp in whiskey and tenderloin in black truffle sauce. Its sophisticated decor is perfect for singles (at the bar) and couples (in romantic thatched mezzanines).

El Coconut (tel. 506/2653-0086, 5–10 P.M. Tues.–Sun.) offers open-air gourmet fusion dining in hip and elegant surrounds. Typical dishes include mussels in creamy brandy sauce ($29.50) and jumbo garlic shrimp ($32).

Another winner for nouvelle dining is **Capitán Suizo** (tel. 506/2653-0075, 7 A.M.–9:15 P.M. daily), where German chef Roland merges European influences into a tropical setting. The creative menu runs from a perfect tomato soup to tilapia with olives, fresh tomato sauce, and macadamia vegetables. I've also enjoyed a curried chicken ($6), corvina in mango sauce ($8), and tilapia in caper sauce ($10). The dinner menu changes daily.

The air-conditioned, glass-enclosed elegant **Carolina's Restaurant** (tel. 506/8379-6834, 6–11 P.M. Thurs.–Tues.) offers a similar variety of superb nouvelle dishes, such as papaya-curry soup ($7) and tuna filet in fresh green spicy sauce ($15). And Chef Tish Thalman's ◖ **Dragonfly** (tel. 506/2653-1506, www.dragonflybarandgrill.com, 5–11 P.M. Mon.–Sat.) delivers mouthwatering fusion dishes, such as Thai-style crispy fish cake with curried sweet corn. You dine beneath canvas, but the place exudes romantic elegance. It's open for dinner only, closes for the month of October, and accepts cash only.

Cordon Bleu-trained Israeli chef Shlomy Koren serves up delicious Mediterranean dishes at **Restaurante Seasons** (tel. 506/8368-6983, 6–10 P.M. Mon.–Sat.), at Hotel Arco Iris. How about stuffed rigatoni with shrimp in a light creamy tomato sauce ($7.50) as an appetizer? And Middle Eastern–style chicken marinated in red wine and spices ($13)? It has a great wine selection and friendly service.

My favorite coffee shop is **Olga's Coffee Shop** (tel. 506/8395-5838, 7 A.M.–7 P.M. Mon.–Sat., 8 A.M.–2 P.M. Sun.), named for the lively and erudite Russian owner. This modern café has walls of glass, free Wi-Fi, and World music. Olga serves granola with yogurt breakfasts, homemade sandwiches, banana bread, and organic salads. Another good bet is the elegant **Coffee Navi** (7 A.M.–10 P.M. daily), outside the Tamarindo Diría hotel, serving quiche, Caesar salad, panini, and cappuccinos. Somewhat simpler, and offering fabulous focaccia sandwiches is **Buon Appetito** (no tel., 6 A.M.–midnight daily).

For groceries, head to **Supermercado Tamarindo** (9 A.M.–5 P.M. daily) or **Super Las Palmeras,** 100 meters east of Hotel Tamarindo Diría.

Information and Services

For tourist information, head to the U.S.–run **Costa Rica Paradise Tour Information** (tel. 506/2653-2251, www.crparadise.com, 8 A.M.–6 P.M. daily), in Plaza Conchal.

Jaime Peligro Bookshop (tel. 506/8820-9004, 9 A.M.–7 P.M. Mon.–Sat., noon–5 P.M.

a sign warns of crocodiles in Tamarindo

© CHRISTOPHER P. BAKER

Sun.) sells used and new books and CDs and also has a book exchange.

In medical need? Call the **Coastal Emergency Medical Service** (tel. 506/2653-1974). There's a **pharmacy** (tel. 506/2653-0210) next to Hotel El Milagro.

The many Internet cafés include **Cyber Bakanos** (tel. 506/2653-0628, 9 A.M.–10 P.M. daily), which doubles as an international call center; and **ILACNET** (tel. 506/2653-1740, 8 A.M.–7 P.M. daily), in Plaza Conchal, which also hosts a bank, the post office, and public toilets.

The **police station** (tel. 506/2653-0283), near Tamarindo Vista Villas, was due to relocate to Plaza Tamarindo in 2009.

The **Wayra Instituto de Español** (tel. 506/2653-0359, www.spanish-wayra.co.cr) offers Spanish language tuition courses.

Getting There and Away

SANSA and **Nature Air** operate scheduled daily service between Tamarindo and San José. The SANSA office is on the main street. A $3 departure tax is collected at the airport.

Alfaro-Tracopa buses (tel. 506/2222-2666) depart San José from Calle 14, Avenidas 3/5, at 8:30 A.M., 11:30 A.M., and 3:30 P.M. ($5). Buses (tel. 506/665-5891) depart Liberia for Tamarindo six times daily 3:50 A.M.–4:10 P.M.; and from Santa Cruz at 4:20 A.M., 5:30 A.M., 8:30 A.M., 10:30 A.M., 1:30 P.M., 3:30 P.M., and 8 P.M.

Return buses depart Tamarindo for San José at 3:30 A.M., 5:45 A.M. (Sun.), and 2 P.M.; for Liberia six times 5:45 A.M.–6:30 P.M.; and for Santa Cruz at 6 A.M., 9 A.M., noon, 2:30 P.M., and 4:15 P.M.

Tamarindo Shuttle (tel. 506/2653-2727) charges $18 for "door-to-door" service from Liberia airport.

Grayline (tel. 506/2220-2126, www.graylinecostarica.com) and **Interbus** (tel. 506/2653-4314,, www.interbusonline.com), in Plaza Conchal, offer shuttles.

There's no gas station, but the **Ferretería**, at the entrance to town, sells gas.

You can rent cars locally with **Hertz** (tel. 506/2653-1358) and **Mapache** (tel. 506/2653-6363).

Getting Around

Bahéa Tamarindo Tours (tel. 506/2653-1987) rents scooters ($39 per day) and mountain bikes ($13 per day).

South to Junquillal

PLAYA AVELLANAS

From Tamarindo, you must backtrack to Villarreal in order to continue southward via Hernández (three kilometers south of Villarreal). The narrow dirt coast road becomes impassable in sections in the wet season, when you may have better luck approaching Playa Avellanas and Lagartillo from the south via Paraíso, reached by paved road from Santa Cruz.

Between Tamarindo and Avellanas, most of the coastline backs onto **Hacienda Pinilla,** which covers 1,800 hectares. This former cattle ranch is one of the most upscale residential resort communities in the country, with a championship 18-hole golf course, trails through a nature reserve with lagoons, a stable for horse rides ($15–35), a small hotel, plus scores of villas and condos for rent. It was still a work in progress at last visit.

Beautiful coral-colored Playa Avellanas, 12 kilometers south of Tamarindo, is renowned for its barrel surf. You can rent surfboards at **Cabinas Las Olas** (tel. 506/2658-9315, www.cabinaslasolas.co.cr).

Avellanas Surf School (tel. 506/2652-9042, www.avellanasurfschool.com) rents surfboards and offers classes and clinics.

Theft and car break-ins are major problems at the beaches. Never leave items in your car!

Accommodations and Food

You can **camp** ($2 pp) under thatch at **Bar y Restaurante Gregorio's.** It also has three basic *cabinas* ($15 s, $20 d) with private baths and cold water. Nearby **Lola's on the Beach** (tel. 506/2658-8097), a rustic beachfront restaurant, is famous for its namesake giant pig and also for dishes such as Hawaiian rawfish salad.

There are several other basic options. The best bet for backpackers is **Blue Trailz** (tel./fax 506/2652-9153, $5 camping, $12 pp), with three bunkrooms and shared bathrooms. There's a bare-bones TV lounge, kitchen, barbecue, and hammocks under thatch, plus an

Argentinian "gourmet" bistro. Surf packages are offered. It rents tents ($6.50).

Swiss-run **Cabinas Las Olas** (tel. 506/2658-8315, www.cabinaslasolas.co.cr, $60 s or $70 d low season; $70 s or $80 d high season) is an "upscale" surfers' place with 10 bungalows widely spaced amid the dry forest. Each has private bathroom, bidet, and hot water. A raised wooden walkway leads 300 meters across mangroves to the beach. The video-bar and restaurant have an appealing ambience. It has ping-pong and rents kayaks, boogie boards, snorkeling gear, mountain bikes, and surfboards.

If you like minimalist contemporary styling you'll like **Las Avellanas Villas** (tel. 506/2652-9212, www.lasavellanasvillas.com, $55 s/d low season, $65 s/d high season), 300 meters inland of the beach. The five self-contained cabins set amid spacious lawns have glazed concrete floors, slightly ascetic yet stylish furniture (including a double bed and bunk), small kitchens, and heaps of light through cross-ventilated French doors opening to wooden decks. A pool was planned. Next door, the six-room **Hotel Mauna Loa Surf Resort** (tel. 506/2652-9012, www.maunaloa.it, $70) offers a similar and perfectly appealing alternative. The impressive **Villas Kaiki** (tel. 506/2652-9060, www.villaskaiki.com, $55–65 low season, $75–85 high season) is a virtual carbon copy of Las Avellanas Villas, 400 meters away.

Hacienda Pinilla (tel. 506/2680-3000, www.haciendapinilla.com, from $120–140 rooms, $295 suites, $300 beach house low season; $145–175 rooms, $325 suites, $395 beach house high season) has a variety of deluxe accommodations, including Superior and Deluxe rooms in the La Posada Hotel, plus a large selection of beach houses and two-, three-, and four-bedroom villas. Here, too, is the lavish, beachfront **JW Marriott Guanacaste Resort & Spa** (tel. 506/2681-2000, www.marriott.com, $299–739 rooms, $999–2,199 suites), which opened in December 2008. It has 310 luxuriously appointed guest rooms, including 20 Junior Suites, all with Wi-Fi and lavish bathrooms. The most sumptuous rooms have their own plunge pools. Plus there's a full-service spa, a huge infinity pool, and four restaurants. The inspiration is old-world colonial, reborn in contemporary vogue.

PLAYAS LAGARTILLO AND NEGRA

Playa Lagartillo, beyond Punta Pargos, just south of Playa Avellanas, is another gray-sand beach with tidepools. Lagartillo is separated by Punta Pargos from Playa Negra, centered on the community of **Los Pargos.** It, too, is popular with the surfing crowd.

About five kilometers south of Los Pargos, the dirt road cuts inland about eight kilometers to the tiny hamlet of **Paraíso,** where another dirt road leads back to the coast and dead-ends at Playa Junquillal.

Pura Jungla Preserve (tel. 506/2652-9160, www.purajungla.com) is an eco-community in the hills one kilometer north of Paraíso. The brainchild of environmentalist Ray Beise, the 235-hectare nature preserve is designed to show that beautiful homes can be built in harmony with their natural surroundings. Ray has returned erstwhile cattle pasture to forest that now draws a plethora of wildlife, including monkeys and cats. There's an exotic fruit orchard, experimental tree farm, organic banana grove, and nature trails, one of which leads to a waterfall.

Accommodations

A delightful Peruvian couple run **Kontiki** (tel. 506/2652-9117, www.kontikiplayanegra.com, $10 s, $20 d, $25 quad), about three kilometers north of Los Pargos, between Lagartillo and Negra. This rustic and fairly basic farmhouse with a wonderful offbeat ambience has five thatched *cabinas* raised on stilts, with shared bath and cold water; one rates as a virtual treehouse and features two dorms with "Goldilocks and the Three Bears"–style bunks and a double bed (howler monkeys hang out in the treetops at eye level). The place abounds

with pre-Columbian figurines. Peruvian dishes are cooked in an outdoor oven, and it has Wi-Fi. Rates include breakfast.

The three-story, all-hardwood **Mono Congo Lodge** (tel. 506/2652-9261, www.monocongolodge.com, $65–95 s/d), about one kilometer north of Los Pargos, has lost its warm welcome of late. This Colorado-style lodge that has been described as "a mixture of Swiss Family Robinson tree house and Australian outback bed-and-breakfast" is hand-built of stone and hardwoods and has six simply furnished air-conditioned rooms with magnificent high beds boasting orthopedic mattresses, mosquito nets, and batik spreads, plus screened windows, TVs/DVDs, and exquisite tile work in the bathrooms (some have stone walls). A wraparound veranda has hammocks and leather lounge chairs. It's surrounded by fruit trees and dry forest. Horseback riding tours, boat charters, and massage can be arranged. Rates include breakfast.

Pablo's Picasso (tel. 506/2652-9158, $12.50 with fan, $15 with a/c), at Playa Negra, is legendary among surfers. This rustic hostelry and surfers' gathering spot is run by a friendly Yank named Paul. He offers four air-conditioned, spacious, and surprisingly elegant rooms with private baths with cold water (two with shared baths), and two air-conditioned *cabinas* with kitchens. You can camp for $4 per person, including toilets and showers. Hammocks are slung beneath the rustic bar, which has free Internet and a pool table.

For an alternative, consider **Pico Negro Surf Camp** (tel. 506/2652-9369, $10 pp), with four rooms in a two-story building facing the village soccer field. Each has shared stoned-lined showers with cold water only, and pizzas are served in a rustic restaurant.

By the sands at Playa Negra, **Hotel Playa Negra** (tel. 506/2652-9134, www.playanegra.com, $70 s or, $80 d low season, $77 s or $88 d high season) is designed like a South African kraal. The circular cabins are lovely, with simple yet colorful motifs. It has a simple restaurant and games room, plus a swimming pool and surf shop.

"Burgers as Big as Your Head" at Pablo's Picasso in Playa Negra

My vote for best digs for miles goes to the Peruvian-run **Café Playa Negra** (tel. 506/ 2652-9351, www.playanegracafe.com, $17–29 s, $30–42 d low season; $20–32 s, $36–48 d high season). This cozy option has expanded and now exudes tremendous ambience beyond the antique-style doors. It has six rooms (two with bunks) appointed with glazed concrete floors, plump sofas, mattresses atop poured concrete with Guatemalan spreads, sponge-washed walls, and hammocks on a broad veranda facing a gorgeous pool. Three rooms are air-conditioned; three have ceiling fans. It also has a full bar, board games, and Peruvian restaurant.

Food

Carlos at **Café Playa Negra** (7 A.M.–9 P.M. daily) conjures superb pancakes, French toast, quiches, sandwiches, ceviche, entrées such as mahi mahi with creamy seafood sauce with shrimp ($9), plus killer *batidos* (shakes). Friday is sushi night. The café also offers Internet connections ($2.50 per hour) and laundry service ($7.50 per load).

Paul, at **Pablo's Picasso** (11 A.M.–until the last guest leaves), serves "burgers as big as your head" ($4), plus pancakes ($3), sandwiches, and pastas.

PLAYA JUNQUILLAL

Playa Junquillal, four kilometers southwest of Paraíso and 31 kilometers west of Santa Cruz, is an attractive, four-kilometer-long, light-gray-sand beach with rock platforms and tidepools. Beware the high surf and strong riptides. The beachfront road dead-ends at the wide and deep Río Andumolo, whose mangrove estuary is home to birds and crocodiles.

Paradise Riding (tel. 506/2658-8162, www .paradiseriding.com) offers horse-riding trips.

Accommodations and Food

Accommodations in Junquillal struggle to draw a clientele, and the scene was fluid at last visit. There are more options than listed here.

Despite its fabulous clifftop perch, the **Iguanazul Beach Resort** (tel. 506/2658-8123, www.iguanazul.com) appeals mainly to Tico travelers, and at last visit the public areas remain in need of a total remake.

Villa Roberta B&B (tel. 506/2658-8127, www.junquillal.com, $35–50 low season, $50–75 high season) is a modern hilltop home about 400 meters inland of the beach. It rents two spacious rooms. One is a very attractive double room with a black stone floor and king-size bed, and a beautiful bathroom with stone floor, sink, and shower. The second is an air-conditioned apartment with lofty ceiling, small kitchen, and a tasteful bathroom with a bidet. Each has a pleasing motif with dark hardwood accents and sea-blue tiles. It has a deep kidney-shaped pool plus hammocks on verandas.

About 100 meters south, a German-Tico couple run **El Castillo Divertido** (tel./fax 506/2658-8428, castillodivertido@hotmail.com, $30 s, $42 d), a crenellated three-story structure with a breezy hillside setting 300 meters inland of the beach. It has six simply furnished rooms with large louvered-glass windows, private bath (three have hot water and ocean view). There's a rooftop sundeck.

The **Hibiscus Hotel** (tel./fax 506/2658-8437, $30 s, $40 d) is set amid landscaped grounds full of palms and plantains and run by a German couple. All five rooms—genteel and spotless—have fans and private baths with hot water, plus hammocks on terraces. Quality seafood is served in a pretty little dining area.

In the center of the beach, the German-run **Villa Serena** (tel./fax 506/2658-8430, www.land-ho.com, $65 s/d low season, $150 high season) has 10 modern bungalows. The spacious, light, and airy rooms—all with fans and private baths with hot water—are spread out among palms and surrounded by emerald-green grass and flowery gardens. The villa has a cozy lounge overlooking the beach, a library, and a swimming pool, and a hibiscus-encircled tennis court. Dinners are served on an elevated veranda overlooking the ocean. It offers spa treatments.

Prefer a bed-and-breakfast inn? **Hotelito Si Si Si** (tel. 506/2658-9021, www.hotelitosisisi.com, $79 s/d room, $99 casita) offers three rooms and a one-bedroom *casita* with king-size beds.

For self catering, try **Plumitas Pacífica** (tel. 506/2658-7125, www.plumitapacifica.com, $85 low season, $95 high season), with two spacious, simply furnished apartment units with full, marble-topped kitchens. They smelled of fresh concrete. It has a tremendous beachfront setting.

For the "The best fish sandwich in Central America," or an early morning espresso, head to **Rudy's** (no tel., 6:30 A.M.–10 P.M. daily), which doubles as the local grocery store. It has themed food nights.

Getting There

A bus (tel. 506/221-7202) departs San José for Junquillal from Avenida 3, Calle 20, daily at 2 P.M. ($5, five hours). Buses depart Santa Cruz at 5 A.M., 10 A.M., 2:30 P.M., and 5:30 P.M. Return buses depart for Santa Cruz at 6 A.M., 9 A.M., 12:30 P.M., and 4:30 P.M.; and for San José at 5 A.M.

Playa Lagarto to Ostional

PLAYA LAGARTO AND SOUTH

South of Junquillal, the dirt road leads along a lonesome stretch of coast to Nosara (35 km south of Junquillal). Fabulous beaches lie hidden along this route, albeit for most of the way out of sight of the road. Until recently, there were few hotels. Just forest, cattle pasture, lonesome rustic dwellings, and an occasional fishing village. Things are stirring here, finally, and several hotels have opened in the past two years.

If driving south from Tamarindo or west from Santa Cruz on the Santa Cruz–Junquillal road, you must turn south at Soda Las Lucas, four kilometers east of Paraíso—the turnoff is signed for Marbella (16 km) and Nosara. *There are several rivers to ford. A four-wheel-drive vehicle is essential.*

About six kilometers south of the junction, the road briefly hits the shore at **Lagarto** before curling inland to **Marbella,** from where a side road runs down to **Playa Lagarcito.** Four kilometers farther you'll pass black-sand **Playa Azul.** About eight kilometers farther south, a turnoff from the coast road leads to the fishing hamlet of **San Juanillo.** Ostional is five kilometers farther south.

Paski Adventures (tel. 506/2652-8086) offers sportfishing out of The Sanctuary resort (tel. 506/2682-8111, www.thesanctuaryresort.com).

Accommodations and Food

Casa Mango (tel. 506/2682-8032, donjim@racsa.co.cr, $12 pp), on a hillside three kilometers south of Marbella, has four handsome yet bare-bones wooden *cabinas* with fans, and shared bathrooms with cold water only; there is also a thatched *casa* with kitchen ($60 up to six people). It has a restaurant and bar with pool table and veranda with rockers.

Upscale travelers might check into **The Sanctuary** (tel. 506/2682-8111, www.thesanctuaryresort.com, $110 s/d rooms, $135–160 cottages low season; $140 s/d rooms, $175–210 cottages high season), a full-blown resort at Playa Azul. It has condos in a gracious contemporary take on colonial plantation style. There's a spa, tennis, swimming pool, and water sports. It no longer operates as an all-inclusive resort.

At San Juanillo, **Cabinas El Sueño** (tel. 506/2682-8074, $35 s/d low season, $40 high season) has 10 colorful, well-lit, simply furnished rooms.

For those who don't mind spartan accommodations, one of my all-time faves is **◖ Tree Tops Inn** (tel./fax 506/2682-1334, treetopscostarica@gmail.com, $125–145 s/d), a secluded and rustic one-room bed-and-breakfast tucked above a cove at San Juanillo. This charming place is the home of former race-car champion Jack Hunter and his wife, Karen—delightful hosts who go out of their way to make you feel at home. You're the only guest. There's one basically furnished room with outdoor shower. As I said, spartan! You're here for the spectacular solitude and setting that includes a horseshoe reef with live coral that's great for snorkeling, and a private beach for an all-over tan.

Monkeys cavort in the treetops. The couple offers turtle safaris to Ostional, a swim-with-turtle excursion, plus sportfishing tours; if you catch your own fish, Karen will prepare sushi. She also fixes gourmet five-course dinners ($34 pp). Rates include a real English breakfast. Reservations are essential.

Another delight is the Swiss-run **Luna Azul** (tel. 506/2682-1400, fax 506/2682-1047, www.hotellunaazul.com, $80 s or $95 d low season, $110 s or $135 d high season), high on a hilltop between San Juanillo and Ostional. Its colorful contemporary aesthetic is appealing, and the views are killer from the mezzanine open-air restaurant overlooking a lovely infinity pool and sundeck. It has seven spacious, cross-ventilated cabins with garden showers. And health treatments are offered. A lovely place!

The hilltop **La Joya de Manzanillo** (tel. 506/8288-9843, www.lajoyademanzanillo.com), new for 2008 at Playa Manzanillo, has six cabins amid lawns on an old *finca*. A circular restaurant has all-around views. The rooms are nothing special, however, and have "suicide showers" (there is an electrical switch in the shower unit over your head). Somewhat more impressive is **Hotel Villa La Granadilla** (tel. 506/8810-8929, http://hotellagranadilla.com, $20 room, $30 suite, $40 apartment low season; $40 room, $50 suite, $60 apartment high season), two kilometers south of San Juanillo. This two-story Spanish colonial-style hotel has three suites, a one-bedroom apartment, and a suite. There's a pool and thatched restaurant.

Most impressive of the newcomers is **Hotel Punta India** (tel. 506/8815-8170, www.puntaindia.com, $100 s/d), with six self-contained, two-bedroom, two-story villas. The lovely layout includes poured concrete sofas with colorful cushions, and furnishings are comfortable and simple. I like the thatched open-air restaurant overlooking a pool.

◖ OSTIONAL NATIONAL WILDLIFE REFUGE

The 248-hectare Refugio Nacional Silvestre Vida Ostional begins at Punta India, about two kilometers south of San Juanillo, and extends

RESPITE FOR THE RIDLEY

Elsewhere in Costa Rica, harvesting turtle eggs is illegal and usually occurs only in the dead of night. At Ostional it occurs legally and by daylight. The seeming rape of the endangered ridley – called *lora* locally – is the pith of a bold conservation program that aims to help the turtles by allowing the local community to commercially harvest eggs in a rational manner.

Costa Rica outlawed the taking of turtle eggs nationwide in 1966. But egg poaching is a time-honored tradition. The coming of the first *arribada* to Ostional in 1961 was a bonanza to the people of Ostional. Their village became the major source of turtle eggs in Costa Rica. Coatis, coyotes, raccoons, and other egg-hungry marauders take a heavy toll on the tasty eggs, too. Ridley turtles have thus hit on a formula for outwitting their predators – or at least of surviving despite them: They deposit millions of eggs at a time (in any one season, 30 million eggs might be laid at Ostional). Ironically, the most efficient scourge are the turtles themselves. Since Ostional beach is literally covered with thousands of turtles, the eggs laid during the first days of an *arribada* are often dug up

by turtles arriving later. Often before they can hatch, a second *arribada* occurs. Again the beach is covered with crawling reptiles. As the newcomers dig, many inadvertently excavate and destroy the eggs laid by their predecessors and the beach becomes strewn with rotting embryos. Even without human interference, only 1 percent to 8 percent of eggs in a given *arribada* will hatch. Meanwhile, tens of thousands of adult ridleys are killed at sea for meat and to make "shoes for Italian pimps," in the words of Archie Carr.

By the early 1970s, the turtle population seemed to be below the minimum required to maintain the species. After a decade of study, scientists concluded that uncontrolled poaching of eggs would ultimately exterminate the nesting colony. They also reasoned that a *controlled* harvest would actually rejuvenate the turtle population. Such a harvest during the first two nights of an *arribada* would *improve* hatch rates at Ostional by reducing the number of broken eggs and crowded conditions that together create a spawning ground for bacteria and fungi that prevent the development of embryos.

along 15 kilometers of shoreline to Punta Guiones, eight kilometers south of the village of Nosara. It incorporates the beaches of Playa Ostional, Playa Nosara, and Playa Guiones.

The village of **Ostional** is midway along **Playa Ostional,** which has some of the tallest breaking waves in the country. The refuge, one of the world's most important sea turtle hatcheries, was created to protect one of three vitally important nesting sites in Costa Rica for the *lora,* or olive ridley turtle (the others are Playa Camaronal, and Playa Nancite, in Santa Rosa National Park). A significant proportion of the world's Pacific ridley turtle population nests at Ostional, invading the beach en masse for up to one week at a time July–December (peak season is August and September, starting with the last quarter of the full moon), and singly or in small groups at other times during the year. Synchronized

mass nestings are known to occur at only a dozen or so beaches worldwide (in Mexico, Nicaragua, Honduras, Surinam, Panama, Orissa in India, and Costa Rica).

Time your arrival correctly and out beyond the breakers you may see a vast flotilla of turtles massed shoulder to shoulder, waiting their turn to swarm ashore, dig a hole in the sand, and drop in the seeds for tomorrow's turtles. The legions pour out of the surf in endless waves. It's a stupendous sight, this *arribada* (arrival). Of the world's eight marine turtle species, only the females of the olive ridley and its Atlantic cousin, Kemp's ridley, stage *arribadas.* Ostional is the most important of these. So tightly packed is the horde that the turtles feverishly clamber over one another in their efforts to find an unoccupied nesting site. As they dig, sweeping their flippers back and forth, the petulant

In 1987, the Costa Rican Congress finally approved a management plan that would legalize egg harvesting at Ostional. The statute that universally prohibited egg harvesting was reformed to permit the residents of Ostional to take and sell turtle eggs. The unique legal right to harvest eggs is vested in members of the Asociación Desarrollo Integral de Ostional (ADIO). The University of Costa Rica, which has maintained a biological research station at Ostional since 1980, is legally responsible for management and review. A quota is established for each *arribada*. Sometimes, no eggs are harvested; in the dry season (Dec.-May), as many as 35 percent of eggs may be taken; when the beach is hotter than Hades, the embryos become dehydrated, and the hatching rate falls below 1 percent. The idea is to save eggs that would be broken anyway or that otherwise have a low expectation of hatching. By law, eggs may be taken only during the first 36 hours of an *arribada*. After that, the villagers protect the nests from poachers and the hatchlings from ravenous beasts.

The eggs are dealt to distributors, who sell on a smaller scale at a contract-fixed price to bakers (which favor turtle eggs over those of hens; turtle eggs give dough greater "lift") and bars, brothels, and street vendors who sell the eggs as aphrodisiacal *bocas* (snacks). Net revenues from the sale of eggs are divided between the community (80 percent) and the Ministry of Agriculture. ADIO distributes 70 percent of its share among association members as payment for their labors, and 30 percent to the Sea Turtle Project and communal projects. ADIO also pays the biologists' salaries. Profits have funded construction of a health center, a house for schoolteachers, the ADIO office, and a Sea Turtle Research Lab.

Scientists claim that the project also has the potential to stop the poaching of eggs on other beaches. It's a matter of economics: Poachers have been undercut by cheaper eggs from Ostional. Studies also show that the turtle population has stabilized. Recent *arribadas* have increased in size. And hatch rates are up dramatically.

Alas, illegal fishing within the marine park boundaries kills hundreds of turtles each year.

females scatter sand over one another and the air is filled with the slapping of flippers on shells. By the time the *arribada* is over, more than 150,000 turtles may have stormed this prodigal place and 15 million eggs may lie buried in the sand.

Leatherback turtles also come ashore to nest in smaller numbers October–January.

You can walk the entire length of the beach's 15-kilometer shoreline. Although turtles can handle the strong currents, humans have a harder time: swimming is not advised. Howler monkeys, coatimundis, and kinkajous frequent the forest inland from the beach. The mangrove swamp at the mouth of the Río Nosara is a nesting site for many of the 190 bird species hereabouts.

Turtle Viewing

You must check in with ADIO (Asociación Desarrollo Integral de Ostional, tel./fax 506/2682-0470, adiotort@racsa.co.cr) before exploring the beach; a guide is compulsory ($10) during arribadas, when an entry fee of $10 is payable at the *puesto* (ranger station) at the southern end of the village, where you check in; you watch a video before entering the beach as a group.

All vehicles arriving at night are requested to turn off their headlights when approaching the beach. Flashlights and flash photography are also forbidden. Personal contact with turtles is prohibited, as is disturbance of markers placed on the beach.

Accommodations and Food

Camping ($3) is allowed at **Soda La Plaza,** which has a portable toilet.

The refuge administrative office (tel. 506/ 2682-0428, $7 pp), at the south end of the village, has a clean modern dorm for volunteers with a two-week minimum stay.

Pacha Mama (tel. 506/2289-7081, www .pacha-mama.org) is a "spiritual-ecological village," or commune, on a hilltop near Limonal at the north end of Ostional, about three kilometers inland. Alas, this community has a long history of offending local sensibilities.

Cabinas Ostional (tel. 506/2682-0428, $12 pp), 50 meters south of the soccer field, has six clean, pleasing rooms sleeping three people, with fans and private baths with cold water. Two newer cabins have lofty thatched ceilings. About 100 meters south, the **Bar y Restaurante Las Guacamayas** (tel. 506/2682-0430, $10 pp) has four small but clean rooms with two single beds, fans, and shared bathroom with cold water only.

At the north end of Ostional is the Hungarian-owned **Hotel Rancho Brovilla** (tel. 506/8380-5639 or 2280-4919, www.brovilla .com, $33–45 s, $53–65 d room, $60–80 apartment, $125–200 *casas*), a hilltop retreat with a splendid setting offering views. It has 12 air-conditioned *cabinas,* each with fans, TV, and a private bath with hot water. It also has two two-bedroom *casas* and a two-bedroom apartment. There's a breezy terrace with a plunge pool and restaurant. Plans include tennis courts, horseback riding, fishing, and turtle tours. Rates include breakfast.

Information and Services

The **ADIO** (Asociación Desarrollo Integral de Ostional, tel./fax 506/2682-0470, adiotort@ racsa.co.cr) office is beside the road, on the northwest corner of the soccer field. Rodrigo Morera, the community leader, is helpful. The **ranger booth** (tel. 506/2682-0400) is 200 meters south of the soccer field, behind the **Doug Robinson Marine Research Laboratory** (tel. 506/2682-0812).

The *pulpería* at the northern end of the soccer field has a **public telephone.** There's a **police station** (tel. 506/8828-2892).

Getting There

A bus departs Santa Cruz for Ostional at 12:30 P.M. (three hours, returning at 5 A.M.); it may not run in wet season. You can take a taxi (about $8) or walk to Ostional from Nosara.

The dirt road between Ostional and Nosara requires you to ford (*vanar* in Spanish) the Río Montaña (about 5 km south of Ostional), which can be impassable during wet season; sometimes a tractor will be there to pull you through for a fee. About one kilometer farther south the road divides: The fork to the left (east) fords the Río Nosara just before entering the village of Nosara and is impassable in all but the most favorable conditions; that to the right crosses the Río Nosara via a bridge and the community of **Santa Marta.**

Nosara and Vicinity

◖ NOSARA

Nosara boasts three of the best beaches in Nicoya, each with rocky tidepools where the seawater is heated by the sun—great for soaking. They are backed by hills smothered in moist tropical forest. **Playa Nosara** extends north from Punta Nosara and the river estuary to Ostional. It's backed by mangroves. *Arribadas* of olive Ridley turtles occasionally occur. More are expected. Tiny **Playa Pelada** is tucked in a cove south of Punta Nosara and has a blowhole at the south and a bat cave

at the north end. **Playa Guiones,** separated from Playa Pelada by Punta Pelada, is a ruler-straight, five-kilometer-long expanse of white sand washed by surf and, hence, popular with surfers. *Beware strong riptides!*

The sleepy village of **Bocas de Nosara** is five kilometers inland from the coast, five kilometers south of Ostional, on the banks of the Río Nosara. It maintains a simple traditional Tico lifestyle but otherwise offers little of appeal. A large foreign community lives four kilometers south of the village, where about 200

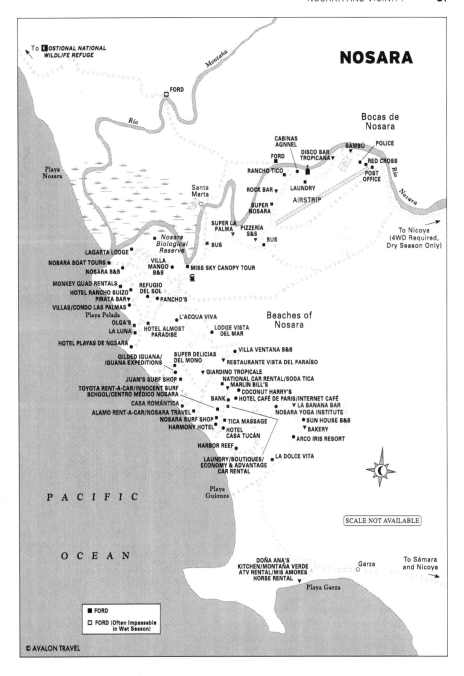

NOSARA

To **C**OSTIONAL NATIONAL
WILDLIFE REFUGE

Montaña

FORD

Río

Bocas de
Nosara

Playa
Nosara

Santa
Marta

CABINAS
AGNNEL

DISCO BAR
TROPICANA▼

BAMBÚ
▼

POLICE

FORD

RANCHO TICO ■

RED CROSS
■

POST
OFFICE

Río

Nosara

ROCK BAR ▼

LAUNDRY

SUPER ■
NOSARA

AIRSTRIP

To Nicoya
(4WD Required,
Dry Season Only)

SUPER LA
PALMA

PIZZERÍA
S&S
▼

BUS

BUS

■ Nosara
Biological
Reserve

■ BUS

Beaches of
Nosara

LAGARTA LODGE ●

VILLA
MANGO ●
B&B

■ MISS SKY CANOPY TOUR

NOSARA BOAT TOURS ■

NOSARA B&B ■

MONKEY QUAD RENTALS ■

HOTEL RANCHO SUIZO ■

PIRATA BAR▼

REFUGIO
DEL SOL ●

● PANCHO'S

VILLAS/CONDO LAS PALMAS ●

Playa Pelada

OLGA'S ●

LA LUNA ■

■ L'ACQUA VIVA

HOTEL ALMOST
PARADISE

● LODGE VISTA
DEL MAR

HOTEL PLAYAS DE NOSARA ●

GILDED IGUANA/
IGUANA EXPEDITIONS

SUPER DELICIAS
DEL MONO

▼ VILLA VENTANA B&B

▼ RESTAURANTE VISTA DEL PARAÍSO

▼ GIARDINO TROPICALE

JUAN'S SURF SHOP ■

NATIONAL CAR RENTAL/SODA TICA

TOYOTA RENT-A-CAR/INNOCENT SURF
SCHOOL/CENTRO MÉDICO NOSARA

■ MARLIN BILL'S

● COCONUT HARRY'S

CASA ROMÁNTICA ●

BANK ● HOTEL CAFÉ DE PARIS/INTERNET CAFÉ

ALAMO RENT-A-CAR/NOSARA TRAVEL ■

▼ LA BANANA BAR

NOSARA SURF SHOP ■

NOSARA YOGA INSTITUTE

■ TICA MASSAGE

● SUN HOUSE B&B

HARMONY HOTEL ●

HOTEL
CASA TUCÁN

▼ BAKERY

● ARCO IRIS RESORT

HARBOR REEF ●

LAUNDRY/BOUTIQUES/
ECONOMY & ADVANTAGE
CAR RENTAL

■ LA DOLCE VITA

Playa
Guiones

SCALE NOT AVAILABLE

P A C I F I C

O C E A N

DOÑA ANA'S
KITCHEN/MONTAÑA VERDE
ATV RENTAL/MIS AMORES
HORSE RENTAL

Garza ○

To Sámara
and Nicoya

Playa Garza

■ FORD

□ FORD (Often Impassable
in Wet Season)

© AVALON TRAVEL

Playa Guiones

homes plus several dozen hotels and restaurants are hidden amid the forest in the area known as the **Beaches of Nosara**. The roads are an intestinal labyrinth.

About 40 hectares of wildlife-rich forest are protected in the private **Nosara Biological Reserve** (Reserva Biológica Nosara, tel. 506/2682-0035, www.lagarta.com) along the river, which harbors caimans and crocodiles.

Entertainment and Events

The nightlife centers in the village, where the most atmospheric bars are **Bambú,** with live marimba on Saturday; **Disco Bar Tropicana,** with disco on Saturday at 9 P.M.; and the **Rock Bar** (tel. 506/2682-0184), with pool tables and five big-screen TVs for Monday night football.

Café de Paris (tel. 506/2682-0087, www .cafedeparis.net) has an open-air movie Friday at 7 P.M. (free).

Sports and Recreation

Nosara Surf Shop (tel. 506/2682-0573, www.safarisurfschool.com) has a "Safari Surf School." It sells and rents boogie boards and

surfboards. **Coconut Harry's Surf Shop** (tel. 506/2682-0574, www.coconutharrys.com) has rentals and surf tours, as does **Corky Carrol's Surf School** (U.S. tel. 714/969-3959, www

NOSARA YOGA INSTITUTE

This nonresidential yoga education center (tel. 506/2682-0071 or 866/439-4704, www.nosarayoga.com) is dedicated to professional training and advanced career development for teachers and practitioners in the field of yoga and bodywork. Perched in the hills behind Playa Guiones, it's the perfect place to relax and recharge. The institute specializes in advanced techniques and offers intensive one- to four-week programs in yoga, meditation, Pranassage (a private one-on-one yoga session, combining yoga assists and hand contact to support clients in deepening their yoga practice), plus nature and health programs.

© CHRISTOPHER P. BAKER

horseback riding at Playa Nosara

.surfschool.net) at Harbor Reef. **Innocent Surf School** (tel. 506/8810-4710, www.innocent surfschool.com) has lessons daily at 8 A.M., 10 A.M., and 2 P.M.

Iguana Expeditions (tel. 506/2682-0259), at the Gilded Iguana, offers sea kayaking and has a surf school. **Fishing Nosara** (tel. 904/591-2161, www.fishingnosara.com) offers sportfishing.

Inevitably, Nosara now has a canopy tour (where doesn't?) at **Miss Sky Canopy Tour** (tel. 506/2682-0969, www.missskycanopytour .com, $60 adults, $40 children), with 21 zipline runs. The longest is 750 meters. Fun! Tours leave at 8 A.M., 2 P.M., and 6 P.M.

Accommodations
UNDER $25
In the village, **Cabinas Agnnel** (tel. 506/2682-0142, $10 pp) offers simple rooms with private baths with cold water.

$25-50
The **Gilded Iguana Resort Hotel** (tel. 506/2682-0259, www.gildediguana.com, $30–65 s/d low season, $45–80 high season) has 12 spacious, cross-ventilated rooms and two-bedroom suites with fans, refrigerators, coffeemakers, toasters, and large walk-in showers with hot water. There's a pleasing bar-cum-restaurant with TV, and sea kayaking is offered.

For grandstand views of both jungle and coast, check into **Lodge Vista del Mar** (tel. 506/2682-0633, www.lodgevistadelmar.com, $36–48 s, $44–56 d), astride a ridge high in the hills overlooking Beaches of Nosara. This three-story modern structure has nine cross-ventilated rooms and one suite, all modestly furnished, with fans, cool limestone floors, and private bathroom with hot water. One has air-conditioning. It has an Olympic-length lap pool, laundry facilities, and a simple outdoor kitchen for guests. Rates include breakfast.

Two similarly priced options are **Harbor Reef Lodge** (tel. 506/2682-1000, www.harbor reef.com), which has four handsomely appointed air-conditioned suites with large sitting rooms and wet bars; and **Pancho's** (tel. 506/2682-0591, www.panchosresort.com), with six cross-ventilated bungalows and a duplex facing a magnificent circular pool.

Opposite Pancho's, and a delightfully colorful option, is **Refugio del Sol** (tel./fax 506/2682-0287, www.refugiodelsol.com, $30 s, $40 d, $55 with kitchen), with four rooms and two apartments along a broad shady terrace with hammocks. The aesthetic is simple yet nice, with ocher and orange color schemes, brass-studded hardwood doors, orthopedic mattresses, ceiling fans, and small modern bathrooms.

Also to consider at Playa Guiones is the Swiss-run **Rancho Suizo Lodge** (tel. 506/2682-0057, www.nosara.ch, $34 s or $50 d low season, $45 s or $63 d high season), with 10 thatched *cabinas* with small but pleasant rooms and private baths with hot water; and **Nosara B&B** (tel. 506/2682-0209, www.nosarabandb.net, $29 s or $39 d low season, $39 s or $49 d high season), which has nice hosts but is a ho-hum property.

Readers continue to complain about the ongoing construction and lack of attention to guests at **Hotel Playas de Nosara,** which cannot be recommended.

$50-100

If setting is foremost in mind, check out **Lagarta Lodge** (tel. 506/2682-0035, www.lagarta.com, $45 s or $50 d low season, $65 s or $70 d high season), atop Punta Nosara and offering stupendous vistas north along Ostional. Four simple rooms are in a two-story house (the upper story reached by a spiral staircase), and three are in a smaller unit with whitewashed stone walls. The latter, with one entire wall a screened window, have mezzanine bedrooms overlooking voluminous open showers and bathrooms. Some have king-size beds. The lodge has a swimming pool and trails leading down to the river and the Reserva Biológica Nosara; boats and canoes are rented ($10). Readers have raved about the meals. Rates include tax and breakfast.

The beachfront **Casa Romántica** (tel./fax 506/2682-0272, www.casa-romantica.net, $60–70 s/d low season, $80–90 high season) appeals for its 10 rooms in beautiful two-story houses with gracious whites and earth tones. Upper rooms are cross-ventilated two-bedroom apartments with kitchens and a wide, shaded veranda. The landscaped grounds contain a pool, *ranchito* with hammocks, and restaurant. It has a tennis court, and you can rent surf and boogie boards. Rates include breakfast.

The attractive **Café de Paris** (tel. 506/2682-0087, www.cafedeparis.net, call for nightly rates) is run by a young French couple who continue to evolve their hotel. It has 12 modestly furnished air-conditioned rooms with ceiling fans, a slanted wooden ceiling with egress for the heat, and private bath with hot water. Rooms vary in size and include a two-bedroom "suite bungalow" with kitchen. There are also five bungalows plus two hilltop villa with suites: they offer fabulous views and each has a spiral staircase to two or three bedrooms. The restaurant is beneath a soaring *ranchito*. Facilities include a souvenir store, the splendid café, a lap pool, pool table, massage, and Internet café.

Run by a delightful French-Portuguese couple, **Villa Mango B&B** (tel. 506/2682-1168, www.villamangocr.com, $49 s or $59 d low season, $69 s or $79 d high season) is a bed-and-breakfast that enjoys views over Playa Guiones. It has four bedrooms with parquet floors, raised wooden ceilings, and large picture windows. It has a kidney-shaped pool (monkeys and coatis come to drink!), plus a delightfully rustic restaurant and sundeck with bamboo rockers and hammocks. It is "lifestyle-friendly." Rates include breakfast and tax.

Also to consider in this price bracket is the new, Mexican-style **Hotel El Ramal** (tel. 506/2682-1060, $40 s, $80 d), with 10 large, simply furnished rooms.

OVER $100

The environmentally sound **Harmony Hotel** (tel. 506/2682-4114, www.harmonynosara.com, $150 s/d rooms, $220–330 bungalows low season; $190 s/d rooms, $270–410 bungalows high season), within spitting distance of the beach, is one of the class acts in Nosara. It offers 24 rooms with king-size beds and simple yet edgily sexy furnishings, as well as 11 one- and two-bedroom bungalows with decks and rinse showers (plus private baths and hot water). Some units have air-conditioning; all have Wi-Fi. The landscaped grounds boast a curvaceous swimming pool, a tennis court, yoga dojo, plus a large bar and restaurant with rattans and bamboos. Rates include breakfast.

A cross-shaped pool highlights the new **Arco Iris Hotel & Resort** (tel. 506/2682-0615, www.samuelcarver.com/Arco Iris.html, $150 s/d), with 10 air-conditioned villas, Wi-Fi, and a Tuscan-style restaurant.

The sensational Balinese-inspired **(L'Acqua Viva Hotel & Spa** (tel. 506/2682-1087, fax 506/2682-0420, www.lacquaviva.com, $185 rooms, $300 suites, $450–600 villas low season; $190 rooms, $325 suites, $500–700 villas high season), which opened in December 2008, has raised the ante considerably at Playa Guiones. Let's start with the jaw-dropping lobby, with a peaked thatched roof and a brilliant contemporary design. Call it tropical post-modernism. Minimalist decor in the 35 spacious, peak-roofed, two-story guest quarters is tastefully contemporary, blending whites with dark Indonesian hardwood pieces, and bold salmons and stylish original art for color. Bathrooms have large walk-in showers. Sunlight pours in through shuttered windows and sliding glass doors, and sensuous bathrooms have coil-shaped showers. The huge trapezoidal pool begs lingering swims, and there's a whirlpool. The bar could well be the hippest west of San José. Lovely! The property is hilly but has ramps plus two units fitted for wheelchairs. There's Wi-Fi in the public areas.

Looking for self-catering? Bibi and Arne Bendixen (tel. 540/2297-8485, www.casa-banda.com) rent lovely apartments of various sizes as **Casa Banda.** And Tiffany Atkinson runs **Nosara Beach Rentals** (tel. 506/2682-0612, fax 506/2682-0153, www.nosarabeachrentals.com).

Food

Marlin Bill's (tel. 506/2682-0458, 11 A.M.–2 P.M., and 6 P.M.–midnight daily, $3.50–13) offers great dining on a lofty, breeze-swept terrace with views. Lunch might include a blackened tuna salad or sandwich, French onion soup ($3.50), and brownie sundae or Key lime pie. Pork loin chops, New York strip steak, and eggplant parmesan typify the dinner menu. The bar has a TV. Next door, **Soda Tica** (tel. 506/2682-0728, 8 A.M.–3 P.M. Mon.–Sat.) is a charming little open-air *soda* serving hot *casados* for $3.

Olga's (no tel., 10 A.M.–10 P.M. daily), a rustic place fronting Playa Pelada, is recommended for seafood ($5 average). Tucked above the beach 50 meters to the south is **La Luna Bar and Grill** (tel. 506/2682-0122, 11 A.M.–10 P.M. daily, $5), an atmospheric place with cobblestone floor and bottle-green glass bricks, and a terrace for dining by sunset. It serves lentil soup, sushi rolls, carpaccio, and more and plays world music from Dylan to reggae.

Café de Paris (tel. 506/2682-0087, 7 A.M.–11 P.M. daily, $4–10) serves crepes, French toast, omelettes, sandwiches such as chicken curry or turkey, and entrées such as penne pasta with creamed pesto fish and duck breast in green pepper sauce, plus 12 types of pizza.

The **Gilded Iguana** (tel. 506/2682-0259, 7 A.M.–midnight daily, $2.50–8) is a favorite with locals and serves super tacos, stuffed jalapeños, tuna salad, seafood, and great shakes. It has live music Tuesday nights. And **Harmony Hotel** (7 –10:30 A.M., noon–3:30 P.M., and 6 –9 P.M., $5–15) is a winner for vegetarian cuisine and fusion cuisine such as coconut basil and ginger jumbo shrimp ($8), and a superb five-spice chicken risotto, although the sushi menu is disappointingly meager.

For Mexican food, head to **Pancho's** (tel. 506/2682-0591, noon–9:30 P.M. daily, high season only), serving all dishes under $8, plus killer margaritas under a thatch roof.

It's definitely worth the snaking drive into the hills to dine at **Restaurante Vista del Paraíso** (tel. 506/2682-0637, noon until the last guest leaves), where you can enjoy sensational views. Debbie, the Texan owner, is a French-trained chef who conjures up the likes of baked goat cheese salad ($8), filet mignon ($19), and Napoleon of beef tenderloin with layers of grilled pineapple and blue cheese ($18).

Information and Services

The Frog Pad (tel. 506/2682-4039, www .thefrogpad.com), in Villa Tortuga, has a book exchange.

Centro Médico Nosara (tel. 506/2682-1212) is in the heart of Beaches of Nosara. Plus, there's a **Red Cross** (tel. 506/2682-0175) in Bocas de Nosara, and a clinic at the west end of the village. The **police station** is on the northeast side of the airstrip field and has no telephone; call the public telephone (tel. 506/2682-1130) outside the station. The **post office** (7:30–11:30 A.M. and 1:30–5:30 P.M. Mon.–Fri.) is next door.

There's a bank next to Café de Paris, which offers Internet service (7 A.M.–9 P.M. daily).

Getting There

SANSA and **Nature Air** have twice-daily service between San José and Nosara.

A Tracopa bus (tel. 506/2222-2666 or 506/2682-0297) departs San José for Nosara from Calle 14, Avenidas 3/5, daily at 5:30 A.M. ($8); the return bus departs from Bocas del Nosara at 12:30 P.M. Empresa Rojas buses (tel. 506/2686-9089) depart Nicoya for Nosara at 5 A.M., 10 A.M., noon, and 3 P.M., returning at 5 A.M., 7 A.M., noon, and 3 P.M.

Budget Rent-a-Car is located at Harmony Hotel (tel. 506/2682-4114).

Interbus (tel. 506/2283-5573, www.inter busonline.com) operates minibus shuttles from San José ($45) and popular tourist destinations in Nicoya and Guanacaste.

There is no direct road link between Nosara and the town of Nicoya. You must drive south 15 kilometers to Barco Quebrado and turn inland; the dirt road meets the paved Nicoya–Sámara road at Terciopelo.

Getting Around

The roads are all unpaved and distances are long. You can rent an ATV for getting around at **Monkey Quad Rentals** (tel. 506/2682-0027, from $50 per day) and **Nosara Surf Shop** (tel. 506/2682-0573, www.safarisurfschool.com, $50 daily).

BAHÍA GARZA TO SÁMARA

The dirt road from Nosara leads south to Playa Sámara (26 km) via the horseshoe-shaped Bahía Garza (8 km south of Nosara), rimmed by a pebbly white-sand beach. Beyond Garza, the road—four-wheel-drive vehicles essential—cuts inland from the coast, which remains out of view the rest of the way.

At **Barco Quebrado,** about 15 kilometers south of Nosara and 11 kilometers north of Sámara, a road heads north uphill to Terciopelo, on the paved Sámara–Nicoya road (en route, you ford the Río Frío). Continuing south from Barco Quebrado on the coast road, you reach **Esterones,** where a side road leads two kilometers to **Playa Buena Vista,** in Bahía Montereyna. Meanwhile, the "main" road divides, north for Terciopelo and south for Sámara (the direct coast road to Sámara requires fording the Río Buena Vista, which isn't always possible; if impassable, take a one-kilometer detour on the Terciopelo road then turn right for Sámara). There are crocodiles in the river estuary.

Sports and Recreation

Fancy a flight in an ultralight plane? Then head to **Flying Crocodile Flying Center** (tel./fax 506/2656-8048, www.flying-crocodile .com, $75–100 for 20 minutes, $120–160 one hour, $170–230 per hour instruction), where Guido, a licensed commercial pilot, will take you up in one of his state-of-the-art ultralights. *Highly recommended!*

Mis Amores Horse Rental (tel. 506/8846-3502, misamores@ice.co.cr), at La Cocina de Doña Ana, offers horseback and ATV rides.

You can try your hand at catching the big one with **Sport Fishing Center Hélios** (tel. 506/2656-8210, www.heliospeche.com), with a fleet of seven boats.

Accommodations and Food

Budgeting backpackers gravitate to **El Castillo** (tel. 506/8824-2822, $15 pp dorm, $20 s, $30 d rooms), at the river mouth at Playa Buena Vista. This Moroccan-inspired freeform house made of river stones has eight rooms with private bathrooms. Campers share bathrooms and toilets in the garden. It has a communal kitchen and rainbow-hued bar.

Sportfishers may appreciate **Hotel Hélios** (tel. 506/2656-8210, www.heliospeche.com, call for rates), at Garza, with eight modern rooms opening onto a pool and lawns. It specializes in sportfishing packages.

You'll fall in love with the German-run **(C Flying Crocodile Lodge** (tel./fax 506/2656-8048, www.flying-crocodile.com, $35 s or $41 d "Pochote", $50 s or $60 d standard, $65 s or $75 d larger unit low season; $43 s or $49 d "Pochote", $60 s or $70 d standard, $80 s or $90 d larger unit high season), between Esterones and Playa Buena Vista. This marvelous spot is an artistic vision with eight exquisite and eclectic cabins spaced well apart in beautifully maintained grounds. Each boasts walls splashed with lively murals, plus hardwood floors, curving concrete bench seats with cushions, a soothing melange of Caribbean colors, and endearing bathrooms boasting black stone floors. The coup de grace is the Oriental Apartment, with a uniquely creative Moorish motif and an imaginative, skylit, freeform bathroom. It also has air-conditioned bungalows with kitchen. A pool has a water swing

and slide, plus there are horses, mountain bikes, motorcycles, and 4WD vehicles. And the Flying Crocodile Flying Center is here.

Next door, **Paraíso del Cocodrilo** (tel./fax 506/2656-8055, www.travel-costarica.net) is a German-run hotel in Spanish neocolonial style and set in wide lawns. Rooms are uninspired but huge.

Perfect for yoga enthusiasts and "counterculture" types, **Alegría** (tel. 506/8390-9026, www.alegria-cr.de, $25 s/d low season, $35 s/d high season), 400 meters toward the coast beyond Flying Crocodile, is a yoga retreat with eight cabin-tents made of bamboo, with woven palm floors, clear plastic A-frame roofs, and mosquito nets and mattresses. They're accessed by a steep trail. It has an open-air kitchen-bar and terrace with astounding views over Playa Esterones. Guests cook for each other and share outdoor "rainforest" showers. The Belgian owner also rents a beautiful wooden home ($60 s/d nightly, $250 per week) with wraparound veranda and gorgeous bathroom. Rates include breakfast and lunch.

La Cocina de Doña Ana (tel. 506/2656-8085, 8–10 A.M., noon–2 P.M. and 6–9 P.M. daily), atop Punta Garza, specializes in seafood; go for the fabulous setting between bays.

Playa Sámara to Carrillo

PLAYA SÁMARA

Playa Sámara, about 15 kilometers south of Garza, is a popular budget destination for Ticos, surfers, and travelers in search of the offbeat. The lure is its relative accessibility and attractive horseshoe-shaped bay with a light-gray beach.

Sámara can be reached directly from Nicoya by paved road (Hwy. 150) via Belén, and you can fly into nearby Playa Carrillo. The village is in the center of the beach. A cattle *finca* divides it from **Cangrejal**, a funky hamlet at the north end of the beach. Playa Sámara extends south about two kilometers to the small ramshackle fishing community of **Matapalo.**

Entertainment

The beachfront **Bar Las Olas,** at the west end of the village, is one of the livelier spots until after midnight, when the crowd gravitates to the no-frills **Tutti Frutti** disco at the Hotel Playa Sámara; the latter is a smoke-filled, sweatbox place and produces a fair share of local drunks, but it's the happenin' dance scene. A more mellow spot, favored by the local Rastafarian crowd, is the rustic yet always packed **La Gondola** (4 P.M.–2 A.M. daily), *the* bar of choice in town; it has darts, ping-pong, and pool. The open-air **La Vela Latina** video-music bar shows big games on a big screen.

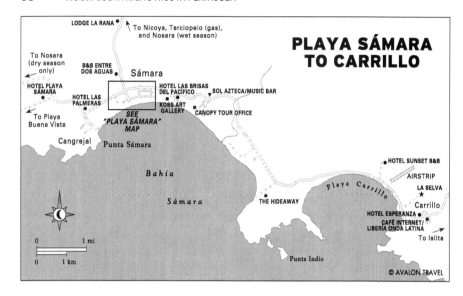

PLAYA SÁMARA TO CARRILLO

Sports and Recreation

Jesse's Surf School (tel. 506/8373-3006, www.samarasurfschool.com) rents surfboards and offers lessons, as does **C&C Surf School** (tel. 506/2656-0628). And **Pura Vida Dive** (tel. 506/2656-0643, www.puravidadive.com) offers dive trips.

Tio Tigre Tours (tel. 506/2656-0098, www.samarabeach.com/tiotigre) has sea kayaking, horseback rides, a dolphin spotting tour, and more, as does **Skynet Tours** (tel./fax 506/2656-0920, info@skynettours.com).

Wingnuts (tel. 506/2656-0153, www.samarabeach.com/wingnuts, $55 adults, $35 children) has a canopy tour.

Accommodations
CAMPING

The swampy **Bar Aloha Camping** (tel. 506/2656-0028, $5 pp) and **Camping Los Cocos** (tel. 506/2656-0496, www.samarabeach.com/campingcocos, $4 pp low season, $5 pp high season, $5 pp camper-van) both play second fiddle to the more appealing **Camping and Bar Olas** (tel. 506/2656-0187, $5 pp camping, $15 s or $25 d huts), with a lively beachside bar and restaurant with shaded campsites with lockers. It also has basic palm-thatch A-frame huts with loft bedrooms.

$25-50

The Italian-run **Cabinas Paraíso** (tel./fax 506/2656-0741, $25 s, $30 d) has four clean, simply furnished rooms with king-size beds, fans, verandas, and private baths with hot water. There's also a large unit that accommodates four people. It rents snorkeling gear and mountain bikes and has a simple open-air eatery. A lesser quality but similarly priced alternative is **Casa Valeria B&B** (tel. 506/2656-0511, fax 506/2656-0317, casavaleriaf@hotmail.com), with eight clean, simply furnished rooms plus four beachfront bungalows.

I like the bargain-priced **Tico Adventure Lodge** (tel. 506/2656-0628, www.ticoadventurelodge.com, $20 s or $30 d low season, $30 s or $50 d high season), made entirely of teak and offering nine rooms in a handsome, sepia-toned, two-story unit with glazed rough-hewn timbers. It also has an apartment and a villa for rent. The C&C Surf Camp is here.

A good bargain, the German-run **Hotel Belvedere** (tel./fax 506/2656-0213, www.belvederesamara.net, $45 s or $78 d room, $65

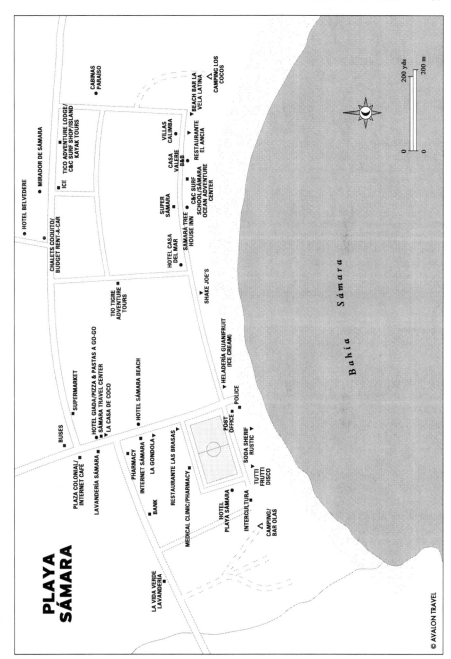

PLAYA SÁMARA

- LA VIDA VERDE LAVANDERÍA
- PLAZA COLONIAL/ INTERNET CAFÉ
- LAVANDERÍA SÁMARA
- BUSES
- SUPERMARKET
- HOTEL GIADA/PIZZA & PASTAS A GO-GO
- SÁMARA TRAVEL CENTER
- LA CASA DE COCO
- HOTEL SÁMARA BEACH
- PHARMACY
- INTERNET SÁMARA
- LA GONDOLA ▶
- BANK
- RESTAURANTE LAS BRASAS ▶
- MEDICAL CLINIC/PHARMACY ▶
- HOTEL PLAYA SÁMARA
- POST OFFICE
- POLICE
- INTERCULTURA
- SODA SHERIF RUSTIC ▶
- TUTTI FRUTTI DISCO
- CAMPING/ BAR OLAS
- HELADERÍA GUANIFRUIT (ICE CREAM)
- SHAKE JOE'S
- TÍO TIGRE ADVENTURE TOURS ■
- HOTEL BELVEDERE
- MIRADOR DE SÁMARA
- CHALETS COQUITO/ BUDGET RENT-A-CAR
- ICE
- TICO ADVENTURE LODGE/ C&C SURF SHOP/ISLAND KAYAK TOURS
- CABINAS PARAÍSO
- HOTEL CASA DEL MAR
- SUPER SÁMARA
- SÁMARA TREE HOUSE INN
- C&C SURF SCHOOL/SÁMARA OCEAN ADVENTURE CENTER
- CASA VALERIE B&B
- VILLAS CALIMBA
- RESTAURANTE EL ANCLA
- ▼ BEACH BAR LA VELA LATINA
- CAMPING LOS COCOS

Bahía Sámara

0   200 yds
0   200 m

© AVALON TRAVEL

s/d apartment low season; $55 s or $90 d room, $75 apartment high season) has 12 pretty, Swiss-style chalets (ranging from doubles to two apartments with kitchens) with attractive bamboo furnishings, mosquito nets, white-washed walls, fans, and private baths with hot water. Some rooms have king-size beds; some have air-conditioning. A stone-walled whirlpool tub sits amid lush gardens and a pool. Rates include breakfast and tax.

Another value-priced winner is the German-run **Bed & Breakfast Entre Dos Aguas** (tel./fax 506/2656-0998, www.hoteldosaguas.com, $40 s or $45 d low season, $45 s or $50 d high season), a charming tropical take on a stone-and-timber Swiss chalet set in a groomed hillside garden, 400 meters inland. It has seven pleasing rooms with rustic wooden furnishings, tile floors, fans, and circular private bathrooms with walls of river stones and hot water. There's a stone bar and a shaded patio. Rates include breakfast and tax. No credit cards.

$50-100

The **Hotel Casa del Mar** (tel. 506/2656-0264, www.casadelmarsamara.com, $30 s or $40 d shared bath year-round, $55 s/d private bath low season, $75 s or $85 d private bath high season), run by French-Canadians, is a relaxing and well-run bed-and-breakfast with 17 modestly furnished rooms with attractive decor, fans, private baths, hot water, and heaps of light through louvered windows (two rooms have a kitchenette). There's a whirlpool tub. Rates include breakfast and tax.

Charm and character pervade **Hotel Giada** (tel. 506/2656-0132, www.hotelgiada.net, $55 s or $65 d low season, $65 s or $80 d high season), with 13 rooms with faux terra-cotta tile floors, sponge-washed ocher and cream decor, bamboo beds (some are king-size), and wide balconies. There's a pool and a pizzeria. Rates include breakfast and tax.

The striking **Mirador de Sámara** (tel. 506/2656-0044, www.miradordesamara.com, $80-95 s/d low season, $90-105 high season) commands the hill overlooking Sámara. German-owned, it sets a high standard. Six

large apartments each sleep five and have full kitchens, plus four new rooms. They're clinically clean, with simple hardwood furnishings and floors, mosquito nets, and balconies. A beautiful pool fed by a water cascade is inset in a multitiered wooden sundeck. A tower contains an open-walled restaurant serving nouvelle cuisine. This property has lots of steps.

Hotel Sámara Beach (tel. 506/2656-0218, www.hotelsamarabeach.com, $55 s or $69 d low season, $89 s or $92 d high season) is a two-story, 20-room complex with private baths and hot water. Rooms are spacious and bright and have air-conditioning, king-size beds, and patios. The hotel has a small swimming pool, plus a bar-cum-restaurant under thatch. Rates include tax and breakfast.

Hotel Las Brisas del Pacífico (tel. 506/2656-0250, www.lasbrisascostarica.com, $65-90 s/d low season, $80-115 s/d high season), about 600 meters south of Sámara, is a German-run hotel with 38 rooms with white-washed stone walls and private baths with hot water (some have a/c; others have fans). Facilities include an open-air restaurant facing the ocean, two swimming pools, two whirlpool tubs, and a shady lounging area under palms. Separate bungalows sit on a hill, with ocean views.

The Hideaway (tel. 506/2656-1145, www.thehideawaycostarica.com, $85 s/d low season, $100 s/d high season) opened in 2008 inland of the very southern end of Playa Sámara. Its stylish, gleaming white modern architecture impresses. The 12 huge air-conditioned guest rooms are in irregular fourplex units and have equally huge bathrooms, pleasant furnishings, Wi-Fi, and most other mod-cons. Meals are served, and there's a scimitar-shaped pool. The delightful owner, Rosy Rios, was planning movie nights on a large flat-screen TV.

Villas Playa Sámara (tel. 506/2656-0104, www.villasplayasamara.com), at the southern end of Playa Sámara, two kilometers south of Matapalo, operates as a time-share for Costa Ricans. For self-catering villas, consider **Villas Kalimba** (tel. 506/656-0929, www.villaskalimba.com).

$100-200

◖ Sámara Treehouse Inn (tel. 506/2656-0733, www.samaratreehouse.com, $85–115 s/d low season, $95–125 s/d high season) is a thoughtful and irresistible addition, and the nicest place in town. Made entirely of glossy hardwoods, the four thatch-fringed tree-house units with open patios (with hammocks and lounge chairs) face the beach; each has terra-cotta floor, bamboo bed, and lively fabrics, plus TV, ceiling fan, delightful modern bathrooms faced with dark-blue tiles, and wall-of-glass oceanview windows. It offers secure parking and a lovely circular pool in the landscaped forecourt, plus a fully equipped, wheelchair-accessible ground-floor apartment.

Lodge Las Ranas (tel. 506/8859-0144, www.lodgelasranas.com, $75 s or $95 d low season, $95 s or $115 d high season), two kilometers east of town on the Terciopelo road, offers a lofty perch. Here, rustic furniture (including canopied log beds) and stylish contemporary elements combine. A serpentine pool studs a hillside terrace.

Food

I breakfast at **La Casa de Coco** (tel. 506/2656-0665, 7 A.M.10 P.M. daily): it has huge omelettes and pancakes, plus lunchtime *casados,* sandwiches, and even chicken curry ($6) at night.

Late risers might opt for breakfast at **Shake Joe's** (tel. 506/2656-0252, 11 A.M.–9 P.M. Tues.–Sun., $3–10), an offbeat hangout with oversize sofas with Guatemalan fabrics, plus rough-hewn tables and hammocks strewn around the gravel courtyard; it serves a French toast breakfast with tuna salad and eggs, plus smoked salmon, salade Niçoise, and ravioli.

The airy **Restaurante Las Brasas** (tel. 506/2656-0546, noon–10 P.M. daily) has heaps of ambience thanks to its effusive use of exotic logs. It serves Mediterranean fare, including gazpacho ($4) and paella ($9), plus surf-and-turf. Similarly, I like the creative menu at the no-frills, thatched, beachfront **Restaurante El Ancla** (10 A.M.–10 P.M. Fri.–Wed., $5–10), serving beef stroganoff, garlic sea bass, and calamari.

When things get too hot, head to **Heladería Era Glacial** (1 A.M.–7 P.M. daily), in Patio Colonial, for ice cream.

You can buy groceries at **Super La Sámara.**

Information and Services

Inter-Travel (tel. 506/2656-0302, 8 A.M.– 8 P.M. daily), in Patio Colonial, is a tour information service that also sells Interbus tickets and has an Internet café. **Internet Sámara** is one block south.

The **post office** and **police** (tel. 506/2656-0436) are by the beach, near the soccer field.

A **medical clinic** (tel. 506/2656-0992) and **pharmacy** (tel. 506/2656-0123) adjoin each other on the north side of the soccer field.

Lavandería Sámara (tel. 506/8870-0448, 8:30 A.M.–5:30 P.M. Mon.–Sat.) offers same-day free delivery for laundry. **La Vida Verde** (tel. 506/2656-1051) competes, using biodegradable soaps and detergents.

Sámara Language School (tel. 506/2656-0127, www.beachspanish.com) offers Spanish language courses.

Getting There

SANSA and **Nature Air** fly daily to Playa Carrillo.

Tracopa Alfaro buses (tel. 506/2222-2666 and 2685-5032) depart San José for Sámara from Calles 14, Avenidas 3/5, daily at noon and 6:30 P.M. ($6.50, five hours). Empresa Rojas buses (tel. 506/2685-5352) depart Nicoya for Sámara from three blocks east of the park 13 times daily 5 A.M.–9:45 P.M. ($1.75).

Buses depart Sámara for San José at 4 A.M. and 8 A.M.

Interbus (tel. 506/2283-5573, www.inter busonline.com) operates minibus shuttles from San José ($35) and popular tourist destinations in Nicoya and Guanacaste.

PLAYA CARRILLO

South of Sámara, the paved road continues over Punta Indio and drops down to coral-colored Playa Carrillo (5 km south of Sámara), one of the finest beaches in Costa Rica. An offshore reef protects the bay. The fishing hamlet of

Playa Carrillo

Carrillo nestles around the estuary of the Río Sangrado at the southern end of the bay.

To check out native animal species that are hard to see in the wild, follow signs to **La Selva** (tel. 506/8305-1610, 9 A.M.–9 P.M. daily, $8 adults, $5 children), inland at the southern end of the beach. This wildlife refuge has coatis, tamanduas, peccaries, agoutis, monkeys, and even jaguarundis. Guided tours are offered at 9 A.M. and 5 P.M.

Café Internet Librería Onda Latina (tel. 506/2656-0434) has miniature golf.

Rick Ruhlow (tel./fax 506/2656-0091, www.costaricabillfishing.com) and **Costa Rica VIP Sportfishing** (tel. 506/2637-7262, www.vipsportfish.com/carrillo.htm) offer sportfishing.

Carrillo Tours (tel. 506/2656-0543, www.carrillotours.com) offers all manner of tours locally and far afield.

Accommodations and Food

I like the U.S.–run **Hotel Sunset B&B** (tel. 506/2656-0011, fax 506/2656-0009, puerto-carrillosunset@yahoo.com, $65 s/d), a beautiful hilltop property with a marvelous wooden deck inset with pool, and an open, thatched bar and restaurant with views. It has eight air-conditioned rooms with solar-heated hot-water showers. Rates include breakfast.

The hillside **Hotel Esperanza** (tel./fax 506/2656-0564, www.hotelesperanza.com, $88 s/d low season, $120 s/d high season, including breakfast) is a family-run bed-and-breakfast set in a delightful garden. Recently remodeled (the new exterior is ghastly), it has seven attractively furnished rooms—some larger than others—arrayed along an arcade. A restaurant, for guests only, specializes in seafood. A new level with five suites was to be added.

Carrillo has garnered several new hotels of late, including the Italian-run **Puerto Carrillo Hotel** (tel. 506/2656-1103, www.puertocarrillohotel.com, $50 s or $65 d low season, $60 s or $75 d high season), with eight air-conditioned rooms with pleasant contemporary furnishings, all with cable TV, and Wi-Fi.

At **Hotel Leyenda** (tel. 506/2656-0381, www.hotelleyenda.com, $105 s/d low season, $125 high season), two kilometers south of

Carrillo, a pleasant contemporary hotel enfolds a courtyard with pool. Decor is a bit uninspired, but standard rooms are spacious and have kitchenettes plus ceiling fan and air-conditioning. There's a "VIP House" ($420 low season, $500 high season) with its own pool. This hotel has come up with a fascinating concept: It provides shuttles to the beach, with mobile portable toilets and showers!

About three kilometers south of Carrillo, **El Sueño Tropical** (tel. 506/2656-0151, www.el suenotropical.com, $45–85 s/d low season, $95–195 s/d high season), now owned by a Tica-gringo couple, is a bargain, and I like the tropical motif throughout this lushly landscaped setting. It has 12 clean, simple, recently renovated air-conditioned bungalow rooms with terra-cotta tiles, queen- or king-size beds, direct-dial telephones, and free Wi-Fi; there is also a suite. The hilltop restaurant has a soaring *palenque* roof. There's a pool and a separate kids' pool. Howler monkeys abound in the surrounding forest. Rates include breakfast.

Getting There

The Nicoya–Sámara buses continue to Playa Carrillo. Or you can fly there daily on **SANSA** and **Nature Air.**

Playa Camaronal to Playa Manzanillo

The extreme southwest shore of the Nicoya Peninsula is one of the most remote coastal strips in Costa Rica. The beaches are beautiful and the scenery at times sublime.

South of Carrillo, the dirt road continues a few miles in good condition, then deteriorates to a mere trail in places. In the words of the old spiritual, there are many rivers to cross. The route can thwart even the hardiest four-wheel-drive vehicle in wet season, or after prolonged rains in dry season. For those who thrill to adventure, it's a helluva lot of fun.

Don't attempt the section south of Carrillo by ordinary sedan or at night, and especially not in wet season unless it's unusually dry—many tourists have had to have their vehicles hauled out of rivers that proved impossible to ford.

PLAYA CAMARONAL TO PUNTA BEJUCO

Playa Camaronal, beyond Punta El Roble about five kilometers south of Playa Carrillo, is a remote three-kilometer-long, gray-sand beach that is a popular nesting site for leatherback (Mar.–Apr.) and Pacific ridley turtles (year-round). It was recently earmarked as the **Camaronal Wildlife Refuge** (Refugio de Vida Silvestre Nacional Camaronal). An *arribada* (mass nesting of turtles) occurred here for the first time ever in November 2006. Officially, you are supposed to visit by night only with a MINAE guide ($4 pp). However, in 2008, when I arrived at the onset of an *arribada,* I was horrified to find hundreds of people being permitted on the beach uncontrolled. Children were touching and even sitting on the turtles, while ignorant adults looked on and laughed. I was even offered eggs for sale. *Don't molest the turtles!*

A dirt road leads south nine kilometers from Camaronal to **Playa Islita,** a pebbly black-sand beach squeezed between soaring headlands that will have your four-wheel drive wheezing in first gear. When heading south from Sámara, follow the signs for Hotel Punta Islita inland via Santa Marta (the road was graded and paved in 2008 and it's no longer a scramble over steep mountains). In dry season you may be able to shortcut the detour by fording the wide Río Ora, which is usually impassable in wet season.

The community of **Islita** is enlivened by the **Open-Air Contemporary Art Museum** (Museo de Arte Contemporáneo al Aire Libre), with houses, tree trunks, and even the police station throughout the village decorated in bright paints and mosaics.

South of the community of Islita, in the

© CHRISTOPHER P. BAKER

ridley turtles during an *arribada* at Playa Camaronal

valley bottom, the road climbs over Punta Barranquilla before dropping to **Playa Corazalito.** The dirt road then cuts inland to the village of **Corazalito** (with an airstrip) and continues parallel to and about two kilometers from the shore. The beach is backed by a large mangrove swamp replete with wildlife.

At the hamlet of **Quebrada Seca,** two kilometers south of Corazalito, a side road leads two kilometers to **Playa Bejuco,** a four-kilometer-long, gray-sand beach with a mangrove swamp at the southern end. The dirt road continues south from Quebrada Seca four kilometers to **Pueblo Nuevo,** where the road from Cangrejal connects with Carmona and Highway 21; a side road leads to the funky fishing community of **Puerto Bejuco,** great for birding. Pelicans, jabiru storks, and other wading birds are abundant, picking at the tidbits to be had as local fishermen cut up their catch. It's as colorful a taste of coastal life as you'll find in Costa Rica.

Less than one kilometer south of Pueblo Nuevo, **Jungle Butterfly Farm** (tel. 506/8822-5674, www.junglebutterfly.com, 9 A.M.–4 P.M. daily, $10 adults, $6 children) offers a treat. Entomologist Michael Mallie has developed scenic trails through his 19-hectare forested mountainside property, which has a butterfly breeding facility. Monkeys and other critters abound. Night tours are offered by reservation.

Carrillo Tours (tel. 506/2656-0543, www.carrillotours.com) offers kayaking in the wetlands behind Bejuco beach ($45).

Accommodations and Food

Villas Malinche (tel. 506/2655-8044, $20 pp), in Pueblo Nuevo, has three nicely appointed, modern air-conditioned *cabinas* with ceiling fans, cable TV, kitchenettes, spacious private bathrooms with hot water, and wide terraces. There's a restaurant.

In 2008, Gwen and Edmund Rhodes opened **Rhodeside B&B and Café** (tel. 506/2655-8006, www.rhodesidecostarica.com, $45 s/d low season, $60 s/d high season), one kilometer south of Pueblo Nuevo. The tiny café (7 A.M.–7 P.M. daily) is a delightful spot to break your journey with a cappuccino and baked goodies, and yummy

© CHRISTOPHER P. BAKER

Hotel Punta Islita

natural breakfasts. The couple was also finishing off four spacious, cross-ventilated rooms with ceiling fans and private bathrooms; two rooms have outdoor showers. They share an upstairs kitchen with terrace and ocean views. There's a stable; guided horseback rides cost $35 per person.

One of Costa Rica's earliest deluxe hotels, **Hotel Punta Islita** (tel. 506/2290-4259, www.hotelpuntaislita.com, $360 s/d rooms, $360 junior suite, $425 casita low season; $275 s/d rooms, $395 junior suite, $450 casita high season) commands a hilltop above Playa Islita. The lobby lounge with thatched roof held aloft by massive tree trunks is open to three sides and looks over a sunken bar and horizon swimming pool melding into the endless blues of the Pacific. Rich color schemes are enhanced by terra-cotta tile floors and colorful tile work, and props from the movie *1492*—log canoes, old barrels, and a huge wrought-iron candelabra. The colony includes 20 luxuriously equipped hillside bungalows in Santa Fe style, eight junior suites (each with whirlpool spa on an oceanview

deck), and five two-bedroom *casitas*. In 2007 they were refurbished in stylish contemporary vogue, with flat-screen TVs, divinely comfortable beds and pillows, and luxury bathrooms. A three-bedroom casita sleeps six people. The elegant 1492 restaurant is acclaimed. A private forest reserve has trails, plus there's a canopy tour, gym, full-service spa, two tennis courts, beach club with water sports, and a nine-hole golf course. The restaurant (7–10:30 A.M., 12:30–3 P.M. and 6–9:30 P.M.) is open to the public (as is the beach club by request), serving such delights as bamboo-steamed mahimahi ($21) and tenderloin filet with gorgonzola au gratin ($28).

Bar Barranquilla (tel. 506/8368-2655, 11 A.M.–midnight daily low season, 8 A.M.–midnight daily high season, $2–12), atop Punta Barranquilla, offers spectacular vistas from its half-moon deck. It serves *comida típica* and seafood.

Information and Services
The **police station** (tel. 506/2656-2052) is beside the soccer field in Islita.

Playa San Miguel

Getting There
SANSA and **Nature Air** fly daily to Islita from San José.

ARZA buses (tel. 506/2258-3883 or 2650-0179) depart Calle 12, Avenidas 7/9, in San José at 6 A.M. and 3:30 P.M. (six hours, $5.30) and travel via the Puntarenas–Playa Naranjo ferry and Jicaral to Coyote, Bejuco, and Islita.

You can buy gas at the house of Ann Arias Chávez, on the southwest corner of the soccer field in Quebrada Seca.

PLAYA SAN MIGUEL TO PUNTA COYOTE
Crossing the Río Bejuco south of Pueblo Nuevo, you arrive at the hamlet of **San Miguel,** at the northern end of Playa San Miguel, reached by a side road. The silver-sand beach is a prime turtle-nesting site; there's a ranger station at the southern end of the beach, plus a turtle hatchery. The beach runs south into **Playa Coyote,** a lonesome six-kilometer-long stunner backed by a large mangrove swamp and steep cliffs. The beaches are separated by a river estuary. The wide Río

Jabillo pours into the sea at the south end of Playa Coyote, which, like Playa San Miguel, is reached by a side road that extends two kilometers north and south along the shore. The surfing is superb.

The Río Jabillo and marshy foreshore force the coast road inland for six kilometers to the village of **San Francisco de Coyote,** connected by road inland over the mountains with Highway 21. Turn right in San Francisco to continue south; fortunately, a bridge over the Río Jabillo now permits passage even in the wettest of wet seasons.

Accommodations and Food
San Miguel: The U.S.–run **Blue Pelican** (tel. 506/2655-8046, $35 s/d downstairs, $45 s/d upstairs), a three-story wooden house on Playa San Miguel, has six charming yet basic rooms with rough-hewn four-poster beds, ceiling fans, and shared bathrooms with cold water only. A large room upstairs sleeps five people; smaller rooms are downstairs, including dorm room. The rustic bar/restaurant (11 A.M.–10 P.M. daily low season, 7 A.M.–10 P.M. daily high season)

serves inviting seafood such as Portuguese seafood stew ($9).

Also at Playa San Miguel the German-run **Restaurante Flying Scorpion** (tel. 506/2655-8080, www.vrbo.com/101715, 11 A.M.–10 P.M. daily, $2–12), serves pizzas, has a 42-inch flat-screen TV, and rents five *cabinas* ($45), a second-floor studio apartment ($75), and two houses ($100–250). Weimeraners abound underfoot! The owners make delicious homemade pastas, seafood dishes, and even ice cream.

Recently upgraded, **Hotel Arca de Noe** (tel./fax 506/2665-8065, www.hotelarcade noe.com, $10 pp bunk, $60 s/d low season, $70 high season), one kilometer farther south on the main road inland of the shore, is an elegant, modern, Italian-run, hacienda-style property with lush landscaped grounds and a large swimming pool lined by mosaic tiles. It has five basically furnished bunk rooms with fans and clean, ample bathrooms (cold water only), plus 10 air-conditioned *cabinas* with lofty wooden ceilings, fans, verandas, louvered windows, exquisite fabrics, and private baths with hot water. A restaurant (8–10 A.M., noon–2 P.M., and 6–9 P.M. daily) is open to the public and serves Italian fare, including pizzas. It rents bicycles and horses and has kayak tours and massage. Rates include breakfast. It closes for the middle of low season.

The best place by far—and a great bargain—is (**Cristal Azul** (tel. 506/2655-8135 or U.S. tel. 800/377-9376, www.cristalazul.com, $145 low season, $175 high season, including breakfast), run by Henner and Zene—delightful hosts. The four thatched, glass-walled, air-conditioned rooms set amid hilltop lawns are gorgeous: charcoal-gray floors, white-and-blue decor, ceiling fans, fresh-cut flowers, handmade beds of glazed hardwood, and huge bathrooms with outdoor garden showers. There's an infinity swimming pool and open-air patio for enjoying hearty breakfasts with spectacular views. Henner is a professional skipper and offers sportfishing. A beach bar and a restaurant were to be added. A two-night minimum applies.

Coyote: In San Francisco de Coyote, **Cabinas Rey** (tel. 506/2655-1505, $8 s, $15 d) has simple

rooms, plus a *soda* serving filling meals, and remarkably, a Wi-Fi hot spot!

Cabinas Coyote Lodge (tel. 506/2655-1162, fax 506/2655-0012, coyotelodge@gmail .com, $40 s/d low season, $60 s/d high season) has six simply furnished air-conditioned rooms around a courtyard with shady veranda. Each has cable TV.

The delightful ship-shaped, beachfront **Barco Nico** (tel. 506/2655-1205, www.barco -nico.com, 4–10 P.M. daily, $5–12), at Playa Coyote, offers gourmet fare, from fajitas and pineapple salad to curry chicken and jumbo shrimp in tequila.

You can drive south along the beach at low tide to reach **Restaurant Tanga** (tel. 506/2655-1107), 100 meters south of the Río Jabillo and tucked beneath shade trees beside the sands. It serves simple seafood and allows camping ($5 pp), with restrooms and showers.

Services
Coyote Online (tel. 506/2655-1007, 2–6 P.M. Mon., Tues., Thurs., and Fri.), in San Francisco de Coyote, has Internet service, including Wi-Fi.

Getting There
ARZA buses (tel. 506/2258-3883 or 2650-0179) depart Calle 12, Avenidas 7/9, in San José at 6 A.M. and 3:30 P.M. (six hours, $5.30) and travel via the Puntarenas–Playa Naranjo ferry and Jicaral to Coyote, Bejuco, and Islita. The San José-Islita buses pass through San Francisco de Coyote at about 11:30 A.M. and 10 P.M. and Playa San Miguel about 30 minutes later. Return buses depart Bejuco at 2:15 A.M. and 12:30 P.M., passing through Playa San Miguel around 3 A.M. and 1:15 P.M. and San Francisco de Coyote 30 minutes later.

PUNTA COYOTE TO MANZANILLO
Playa Caletas, immediately south of Punta Coyote and some five kilometers south of San Francisco de Coyote, can also be reached from Highway 21 (on the east side of the Nicoya Peninsula) via Jabillo and the community of La

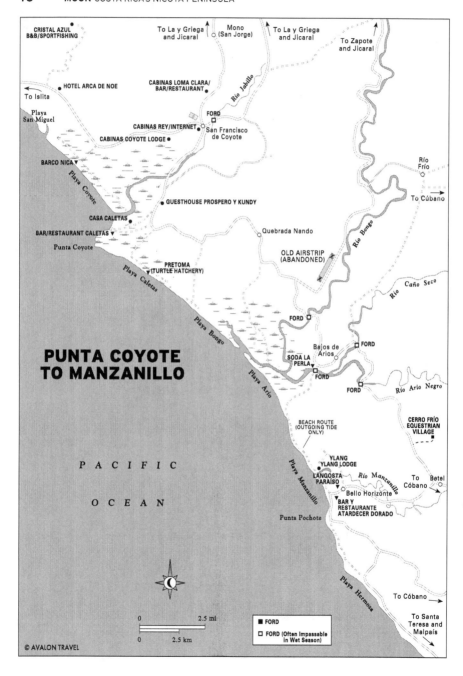

CRISTAL AZUL
B&B/SPORTFISHING

To La y Griega
and Jicaral

Mono
(San Jorge)

To La y Griega
and Jicaral

To Zapote
and Jicaral

HOTEL ARCA DE NOE

To Islita

CABINAS LOMA CLARA/
BAR/RESTAURANT

Río Jabillo

Playa
San Miguel

FORD

CABINAS REY/INTERNET

San Francisco
de Coyote

Río
Frío

CABINAS COYOTE LODGE

BARCO NICA

Playa Coyote

To Cúbano

GUESTHOUSE PROSPERO Y KUNDY

CASA CALETAS

Quebrada Nando

Río Bongo

BAR/RESTAURANT CALETAS

Punta Coyote

OLD AIRSTRIP
(ABANDONED)

Caño Seco

PRETOMA
(TURTLE HATCHERY)

Playa Caletas

Río

Playa Bongo

FORD

PUNTA COYOTE
TO MANZANILLO

Bajos de
Arios

FORD

SODA LA
PERLA

FORD

Playa Ario

FORD

Río Ario Negro

CERRO FRÍO
EQUESTRIAN
VILLAGE

P A C I F I C

BEACH ROUTE
(OUTGOING TIDE
ONLY)

O C E A N

YLANG
YLANG LODGE

Playa Manzanillo

LANGOSTA
PARAISO

Río Manzanillo

To
Cóbano

To Betel

Bello Horizonte

BAR Y
RESTAURANTE
ATARDECER DORADO

Punta Pochote

Playa Hermosa

To Cóbano

N

0   2.5 mi

0   2.5 km

To Santa
Teresa and
Malpaís

■ FORD
□ FORD (Often Impassable
   in Wet Season)

© AVALON TRAVEL

y Griega. This miles-long, brown-sand beach has no settlements. Nothing! It's just you and the turtles that come ashore to lay eggs. The beach is considered the second most important nesting site for leatherback turtles in the eastern Pacific Ocean. **Programa Restauración de Tortugas Marinas** (PRETOMA, tel. 506/2241-5227, www.tortugamarina.org) has a turtle hatchery here and is pushing for creation of the **Playa Caletas-Ario National Wildlife Refuge** (alas, local landowners aren't sympathetic). Ridleys come ashore singly July–March; leatherbacks arrive December–March. Volunteers are needed.

Playa Caletas—a great surfing beach—extends southward into **Playa Bongo, Playa Ario,** and **Playa Manzanillo**—together forming a 12-kilometer-long expanse of sand broken by the estuaries of the Río Bongo and Río Ario, inhabited by crocodiles. Once while driving this road at night, I came around a bend to find a crocodile plodding across the road! Marshy shore flats force the coast road inland.

The route between Caletas and Manzanillo is a true adventure and a high-ground-clearance four-wheel-drive vehicle is absolutely essential in wet season, when the Bongo, Caño Seco, and Ario rivers are often impassable, forcing you over the mountains to Jicaral, on Highway 21 (and thence around the eastern seaboard of the Nicoya Peninsula via Paquera and Tambor) to reach Manzanillo—a five-hour journey! (A shorter, but still challenging route, is to head inland toward Jicaral but cut east to the hamlet of **Río Frío,** which is signed. From here, you can strike east for Cóbano, which is signed beside the soccer field in in Rio Frio. This route, however, may also be impassable, as you have to ford the Río Ario. A second, unsigned, route to Cóbano is signed in Río Frio for Bajo de Ario; after 1.5 kilometers, turn left off this road at a Y-fork, from where a really rugged, little-trafficked road leads to Cóbano and also involves fording the Río Ario.)

South of Caletas, keep straight via the hamlet of **Quebrada Nando** until you reach a major Y-fork by a field. Turn right (if you miss the junction you'll know it, as you'll soon come to

a 90-degree left turn, then run along a disused airstrip) for the Río Bongo. The river crossing is tricky, often with dangerously deep channels (they change yearly with each rainy season; floods in 2008 entirely rerouted the river). If the way across isn't clear, wait for a local to show you the way.

Once across, it's about two kilometers to Soda La Perla (a good place to check local conditions), where the dirt road veers left. About one kilometer along you must ford the Río Caño Seco, another challenge that requires scouting before crossing. Shortly beyond, you reach the 30-meter-wide Río Ario Negro. Again, you may need to wait for a local to arrive and show you the way.

About five or so kilometers farther, turn right at the only junction, just before the hamlet of **Betel.** The descent will deposit you by the shore at **Bello Horizonte,** a small fishing hamlet inland of Playa Manzanillo. South of Bello Horizonte, the tenuous coast road (a devil in wet season) leads over **Punta Pochote** and alongside **Playa Hermosa** to Playa Santa Teresa and Malpaís.

Alternately, from Soda La Perla you can follow a minor dirt road that leads down to Playa Ario; you'll have to ford the Río Ario en route. You can then drive four kilometers along the beach to Playa Manzanillo, where you meet the main road as it comes back to the coast. *Do not attempt to drive along Playa Ario except on an outgoing tide.*

A 1,114-hectare refuge, **Hacienda La Esperanza,** was being created in the Valle de Río Ario at last visit. It will include a butterfly garden, frog garden, and arboretum.

Accommodations and Food

In Bello Horizonte, several no-frills budget *cabinas* include **Bar y Restaurante Atardecer Dorado** (tel. 506/8360-9377), with two basic rooms with bed only (and funky outhouse toilets) for $12 per person. The bar (with TV and jukebox) is a lively center for locals. It serves filling meals; try the *filete al ajillo* (garlic fish, $6).

For comfort head to the Polynesian-style

Ylang Ylang Lodge (tel. 506/8359-2616, www.lodgeylangylang.com, $130 s or $150 d low season, $150 s or $170 d high season), run by a charming Italian woman. It has a TV lounge and small restaurant, a pool studs a huge wooden sundeck, and a suspension bridge leads to forest trails. The five breeze-swept, bi-level hilltop cabins are marvelous, with vast ocean views. Below, patios have swing seats and hammocks and huge walk-in showers; upstairs the huge bedrooms have king-size beds and French doors open to large balconies. One cabin has a kitchen.

The gorgeous (**Casa Caletas** (tel. 506/2655-1271, www.casacaletas.com, $130–165 s/d low season, $165–200 high season) occupies a working cattle hacienda on the south bank of the Río Jabillo. The luxurious rooms feature travertine floors and bathrooms, halogen lighting, rustic glazed hardwood king beds with high-thread-count linens and are cross-lit through sliding glass doors with river-mouth views. Some have loft bedrooms. An invitingly hip breeze-swept bar under thatch opens to the sundeck with kidney-shaped infinity pool, and the lounge with poured concrete sofas with classy fabrics is a delightful place to relax. It offers horseback rides and air-boat river trips.

For simple seafood at bargain prices, head to **Langosta Paraíso** (no tel., 11 A.M.–9 P.M.), a simple *soda* in Bello Horizonte, with fresh lobster for about $10.

Southeast Nicoya

HIGHWAY 21: CARMONA TO PLAYA NARANJO

Highway 21 winds south along the eastern shore of the Gulf of Nicoya via Jicaral to Playa Naranjo, beyond which it swings south around the Nicoya Peninsula bound for Paquera, Montezuma, and Malpaís. When I last drove it, the road was partially paved, with large sections worn to the bone.

Playa Naranjo is one of two terminals for the Puntarenas ferry (Coonatramar Ferry, tel. 506/2661-1069, www.coonatramar.com); use the Naranjo ferry to access the beaches of northern and central Nicoya only. There's a gas station and supermarket here.

Inland of Jicaral, the **Karen Mogensen Wildlife Reserve** (tel. 506/2650-0607) protects 730 hectares of tropical moist forest; to get there, turn off at Lepanto, 11 kilometers south of Jicaral. The **Costa Rican Association of Community-Based Rural Tourism** (ACTUAR, tel. 506/2248-9470, www.actuarcostarica.com; two-day packages $68) arranges accommodation at Cerro Escondido, a lovely simple community lodge with four cabins, plus horseback rides, trails, an orchid garden, and small eco-museum.

Isla Chira

Costa Rica's second-largest island, Isla Chira floats below the mouth of the Río Tempisque, at the north end of the Gulf of Nicoya. It is surrounded by mangroves popular with pelicans and frigate birds, and uninhabited except for a few fishermen, farmers and others who eke out a living from *salinas* (salt pans). Roseate spoonbills and other wading birds pick among the pans.

Isla de Chira Amistad Lodge (tel./fax 506/2661-3261, or c/o Costa Rican Association of Community-Based Rural Tourism, tel. 506/2248-9470, www.actuarcostarica.com, $33–36 pp) offers a simple dorm and six quad rooms. ACTUAR offers packages with boat trips.

Isla San Lucas National Wildlife Refuge

Refugio Nacional de Via Silvestre Isla San Lucas (615 hectares), five kilometers offshore of Naranjo, seems a pleasant palm-fringed place where you might actually *wish* to be washed ashore and languish in splendid sun-washed isolation. Yet a visit to Isla San Lucas once amounted to an excursion to hell.

Until a few years ago, this was the site of the most dreaded prison in the Costa Rican penal system, with a legacy dating back 400 years. In the 16th century, the Spanish conquistador Gonzalo Fernandez Oviedo used San Lucas as a concentration camp for local Chara people, who were slaughtered on the site of their sacred burial grounds. The Costa Rican government turned it into a detention center for political prisoners in 1862. In 1991, it closed. There are still guards here, but today their role is to protect the island's resident wildlife from would-be poachers. It also has eight pre-Columbian sites.

In 2008, the prison was to be restored as a museum. Should you visit the grim bastion, the ghosts of murderers, miscreants, and maltreated innocents will be your guides. A cobbled pathway leads to the main prison building. The chapel has become a bat grotto, and only graffiti remains to tell of the horror and hopelessness, recorded by ex-convict José León Sánchez in his book, *La Isla de los Hombres Solos* (The Isle of the Lonely Men).

Coontramar (tel. 506/2661-1069, www .coonatramar.com/paq_sanluca_es.php, $60) offers tours from Puntarenas.

You can also rent motorboats through the Costa Rica Yacht Club (tel. 506/2661-0784), in Puntarenas, or Oasis del Pacífico (tel. 506/2641-8092) in Playa Naranjo.

Accommodations and Food

The nicest of several accommodations at Playa Naranjo is the modern, Italian-owned **Hotel El Ancla** (tel. 506/2641-3885, $40 s/d fan, $45 s/d a/c), just 200 meters from the ferry terminal, with nine brightly decorated, air-conditioned rooms fronted by a wide porch with hammocks. There's a pool and thatched bar and pizza restaurant where movies are shown at 8 P.M.

PAQUERA AND VICINITY

Paquera, 24 kilometers south of Playa Naranjo, is where the Paquera ferry (Ferry Naviera Tambor, tel. 506/2661-2084, ferrypeninsular@ racsa.co.cr) arrives and departs to/from Puntarenas. The ferry berth is three kilometers

northeast of Paquera. Paquera has banks and a gas station.

Note: If driving south from Playa Naranjo to Paquera, note that this unpaved section is very hilly, with tortuous switchbacks. It's a despairingly rugged ride: the 2009 national budget includes money to pave this section. No buses run this route. At least you get some marvelous views out over the Gulf of Nicoya—including toward Isla Guayabo, which comes into view about six kilometers south of Playa Naranjo, where the road briefly meets the coast at **Gigante,** at the north end of **Bahía Luminosa,** also called Bahía Gigante.

Offshore, **Islas Guayabo and Negritos Biological Reserves** protect nesting sites of the brown booby, frigate bird, pelican, and other seabirds, as well as the peregrine falcon. They are off-limits to visitors.

Dolphins and whales are often sighted offshore (January is the best month for whales).

Tiny **Isla Gitana,** in the middle of Bahía Luminosa, was once a burial site for local peoples (hence its other name, Isla Muertos—Island of the Dead—by which it is marked on maps). The undergrowth is wild, and cacti abound, so appropriate footwear is recommended. You can hire a boat on the mainland beach. You can also reach the island by sea kayak from Bahía Gigante, a 30-minute paddle journey.

Curú National Wildlife Refuge

The Curú Refugio Nacional de Vida Silvestre (tel. 506/2641-0100, www.curu.org, 7 A.M.–3 P.M. daily, $10 adults, $5 children) forms part of a 1,496-hectare cattle *finca*, two-thirds of which is preserved as primary forest. It is tucked in the fold of Golfo Curú, four kilometers south of Paquera, and is part privately owned. The reserve includes 4.5 kilometers of coastline with a series of tiny coves and three beautiful white-sand beaches—Playas Curú, Colorada, and Quesera—nestled beneath green slopes. Olive ridley and hawksbill turtles nest on the crystalline beaches. Mangrove swamps extend inland along the Río Curú, backed by forested hills. Monkeys are almost always playing in the treetops by the gift store, and agoutis, sloths, anteaters, and even ocelots are commonly seen. The facility has a macaw reintroduction program and a reproduction and rehabilitation program for endangered spider monkeys; you can spy them living freely behind an electrified fence (the trail to the enclosure is boggy, so bring appropriate footwear).

Trails range from easy to difficult. You can rent horses ($10 per hour). Guided tours are offered (your tip is their pay). The bus between Paquera and Cóbano passes the unmarked gate. Ask the driver to let you off.

It has basic cabins ($8 pp) and serves meals.

Turismo Curú (tel. 506/2641-0004, turismo curu@yahoo.com) offers snorkeling, kayaking, and scuba diving.

Accommodations

Cabinas y Restaurante Ginana (tel. 506/ 2641-0119, $33 s, $38 d), in Paquera, has 28 simply furnished rooms, some air-conditioned; all have private baths. The restaurant serves hearty local dishes.

You can also bunk in basic rooms with private cold water-only bathrooms at **Curú National Wildlife Refuge** ($35 pp, including meals). Bring a flashlight, as generator-powered electricity shuts down at night.

◖ ISLA TORTUGA

This stunningly beautiful, 320-hectare island lies three kilometers offshore of Curú. Tortuga is as close to an idyllic tropical isle as you'll find in Costa Rica. The main attraction is a magnificent white-sand beach lined with coconut palms. Tortuga is a favorite destination of excursion boats. Cruises depart Puntarenas and Los Sueños marina, at Playa Herradura, near Jacó. It's a 90-minute journey aboard any of a half dozen cruise boats. The cruise is superbly scenic, passing the isles of Negritos, San Lucas, Gitana, and Guayabo. En route you may spot manta rays or pilot whales in the warm waters. Even giant whale sharks have been seen basking off Isla Tortuga. You'll normally have about two hours on Isla Tortuga, with a buffet lunch served on the beach, plus options for sea

kayaking, snorkeling, volleyball, and hiking into the forested hills. It can get a bit cramped on weekends.

I recommend **Calypso Cruises** (tel. 506/ 2256-2727 or U.S. tel. 866/887-1969, www .calypsocruises.com), which runs daily trips from Puntarenas aboard the luxurious *Manta Raya* catamaran with full bar, a fishing platform, and two whirlpool tubs. Trips depart from Puntarenas ($109 low season, $119 high season, including transfer from San José).

The company also has cruises to **Punta Coral Private Reserve** (www.puntacoral .com), where snorkeling, sea kayaking, and other activities are offered, and monkeys and other animals abound in the adjacent forest, with trails. It offers "Paradise Weddings" in a South Seas setting.

Bay Island Cruises (tel. 506/2258-3536, www.bayislandcruises.com) offers cruises yearround aboard the *Bay Princess,* an ultramodern 16-meter cruise yacht with room for 70 passengers. The ship has a sundeck and music, and cocktails and snacks are served during the cruise. And 2008 saw the introduction of a sleek new 200-passenger catamaran with Jacuzzi. Trips depart Los Sueños marina, near Jacó.

TAMBOR

Tambor, 18 kilometers southwest of Paquera, is a small fishing village fronted by a gray-sand beach in **Bahía Ballena** (Whale Bay), a deep-pocket bay rimmed by **Playa Tambor** and backed by forested hills. I find the setting unappealing, but many readers report enjoying Tambor.

You can play a round of golf or tennis at the nine-hole **Tango Mar Golf Club** (tel. 506/2683-0001, www.tangomar.com). Play is free for guests; others pay a $25 greens fee ($15 club rental). Tango Mar also offers tours, sportfishing, and horseback riding.

Ultralight tours (tel. 506/2683-0480) from the Los Delfines airstrip give a fantastic bird's-eye view of the area.

Seascape Kayak Tours (tel. 506/2747-1884, www.seascapekayaktours.com) offers sea kayaking.

© CHRISTOPHER P. BAKER

Tambor ferry to Paquera, Puntarenas

Accommodations

Budget hounds might try **Cabinas y Restaurante Cristina** (tel. 506/2683-0028, eduardon@racsa.co.cr, $20 s/d with shared bath, $22 s or $27 d private bath, $35 *casita*), with nine simply furnished but clean and adequate rooms with fans and cold water only. It also has an air-conditioned *casita* with kitchen, sleeping four people.

I like the flame-orange **Hotel Costa Coral** (tel. 506/2683-0105, www.hotelcostacoral .com, $80 s/d weekdays, $95 s/d Fri.–Sat. low season; $105 Sun.–Thurs., $120 Fri.–Sat. high season), a colorful little beauty of a hotel on the main road in Tambor. It has six air-conditioned rooms in three two-story Spanish-colonial structures arrayed around an exquisite pool with whirlpool. The charming decor includes wrought iron, potted plants, climbing ivy, ceramic lamps, and a harmonious ocher-and-blue color scheme. The upstairs restaurant offers ambience and good cuisine, and its gift store is splendidly stocked.

Another lovely property is **Villas de la Bahía** (tel. 506/2683-0560, http://villasdelabahiacr .com, $30–65 s/d), with two-story villas painted in tropical ice cream pastels.

The architecturally dramatic **Tambor Tropical** (tel. 506/2683-0011 or U.S. tel. 866/ 890-2537, www.tambortropical.com, $140–190 s/d year-round) is a perfect place to laze in the shade of a swaying palm. Ten hand-crafted two-story hexagonal *cabinas* (one unit upstairs, one unit down) face the beach amid lush landscaped grounds with an exquisite pool and whirlpool tub. The rooms are graced by voluminous bathrooms with deep-well showers, wraparound balconies, and fully equipped kitchens. Everything is handmade of native hardwoods, all of it lacquered to a nautical shine. A restaurant serves international cuisine. Snorkeling and horseback riding are offered. Rates include breakfast.

My favorite hostelry hereabouts is the Belgian-run **Tango Mar** (tel. 506/2683-0001, www.tangomar.com, $170 s/d room, $225 suite, $400–899 villas low season; $190 s/d room, $240 suite, $450–999 villas high season), five kilometers southwest of Tambor. It enjoys a beautiful beachfront setting backed by hectares of beautifully tended grounds splashed with bougainvillea and hibiscus. In 2007 rooms received a much needed and more stylish refurbishment, and in late 2008 the public spaces were being totally remade, and conference facilities and a spa were being added. It has 25 rooms, including five Polynesian-style thatched octagonal bamboo Tiki Suites raised on stilts, 18 spacious oceanfront rooms with large balconies, and 12 Tropical Suites with romantic four-poster beds with gauzy netting. You can also choose four- and five-person luxury villas ($400–900 low season, $450–999 high season). It has two swimming pools (one a lovely, freeform, multitiered complex), a nine-hole golf course, stables, water sports, Internet, plus massage and yoga. It rents 4WD vehicles. Rates include American breakfast.

If all-inclusive package resorts are your thing, consider the controversial **Barceló Playa Tambor Resort & Casino** (tel. 506/2683-0303, www.barcelo.com), with 402 rooms sprawling across a 2,400-hectare site. The sibling **Barceló Los Delfines Golf & Country Club** (same contact information), adjacent, comprises 64 Spanish-style, two-bedroom air-conditioned villas arrayed in military camp fashion around a nine-hole golf course.

Food

Restaurant Cristina (tel. 506/2683-0028, 8 A.M.–9 P.M. daily) proffers good seafood and pastas on a shady patio for those on a budget.

The **Restaurante Arrecife** (11 A.M.–2 P.M. and 6–10 P.M. daily low season, 11 A.M.–11 P.M. daily high season, $4–9), in the Hotel Costa Coral, is a charmer with its lively color scheme, and dishes such as ceviche, club sandwich, burgers, fettucine, chicken with orange sauce, and sea bass with heart-of-palm sauce. It has a large-screen TV and karaoke.

New in 2008, the roadside **Trattoria Mediterranea** (tel. 8821-7357, 5:30–10:30 P.M. Wed.–Sun.) has a special pizza Sunday.

The elegant new restaurant at **Tango Mar** (6:30–10 A.M., 11:30 A.M.–3:30 P.M., and 6:30–10 P.M. daily, $4.50–22), under construction at last visit, promises fine dining when completed.

Information and Services

Internet Kara (tel. 506/2683-0001) and a **pharmacy** (tel. 506/2683-0581) are above the roadside **Toucan Boutique.**

Budget Rent-a-Car (tel. 506/2683-0500) and **Tambor Adventures & Tours** (tel. 506/2683-0579) are here also.

Getting There

SANSA and **Nature Air** fly daily to Tambor from San José, with connecting service to other resorts.

Southern Nicoya

CÓBANO

Cóbano, a crossroads village 25 kilometers southwest of Paquera, is the gateway to Malpaís and to Montezuma (5 km) and Cabo Blanco Absolute Nature Reserve. Buses for Malpaís and the Paquera ferry depart from here.

The **police station** (tel. 506/2642-0770) and post office are 200 meters east of the bank; there are public telephones in front of the bank. The **medical clinic** (tel. 506/8380-4125) and **pharmacy** (tel. 506/2642-0685) are 100 meters south of the bank.

MONTEZUMA

Montezuma is a charming beachside retreat popular with budget-minded backpackers and counterculture travelers seeking an offbeat experience. Business owners are prone to shut up shop on a whim—sometimes for days at a time, or longer.

The fantastic beaches east of Montezuma are backed by forest-festooned cliffs from which streams tumble down to the sands. Monkeys frolic in the forests. *Beware riptides!* The **Nicolas Weissenburg Absolute Reserve**

Playa Montezuma

(Reserva Absoluta Nicolas Weissenburg) was created in 1998 to protect the shoreline and forested hills to the east of Montezuma. It's strictly off-limits, however.

The waterfall and swimming hole two kilometers southwest of town (the trail leads upstream from the Restaurante La Cascada) is dangerous. *Do not climb or jump from the top of the fall. Several lives have been lost this way.*

The **Montezuma Butterfly Garden** (tel. 506/2642-1317, www.montezumagardens.com, 8 A.M.–4 P.M. daily, $8 entrance), west of the village, 0.5 kilometers above the Montezuma Waterfall Canopy del Pacífico tour, has a netted garden and breeds morphos and other butterflies species.

Entertainment and Events

Although hard to imagine, this tiny hamlet now hosts the **Montezuma International Film Festival** (www.montezumafilmfestival.com), created in 2007, each November.

El Sano Banano restaurant shows movies nightly at 7:30 P.M. (free with dinner or $6 minimum order).

Sports and Recreation

Montezuma Travel Adventures (tel. 506/2642-0808, www.montezumatraveladventures.com) offers all manner of activities, from ATV tours and horseback riding to its **Montezuma Waterfall Canopy del Pacífico,** which offers tours by zipline between the treetops at 8 A.M., 10 A.M., 1 P.M. and 3 P.M. ($35).

Montezuma Expeditions (tel. 506/2642-0919, www.montezumaexpeditions.com) similarly offers a wide range of tours and activities, as do **Montezuma Eco-Tours** (tel. 506/2642-0467, www.playamontezuma.net/ecotours.htm); **Zuma Tours** (tel. 506/2642-0024, www.zumatours.net); and **Chico's Tour** (tel. 506/2642-0556), which specializes in trips to Isla Tortuga ($40 pp).

Montezuma Yoga (tel. 506/2642-0076, www.montezumayoga.com) at Hotel Los Mangos offers yoga classes at 9:30 A.M. Sunday–Friday ($12).

For horse-riding, the best stable is at **Finca Los Caballos** (tel. 506/2642-0124, www.naturelodge.net, $20 pp per hour), which has mountain and beach rides.

Accommodations

There are many more options than can be listed here.

CAMPING

You can camp at **Chinamo** (tel. 506/2642-1000, $5 pp), which rents tents and equipment.

UNDER $25

There's little to choose from between the mostly uninspired low-end properties, all with basic rooms with shared bathrooms with cold water for around $5 per person.

Budgeting backpackers should check in to **Mochila Inn** (tel. 506/2642-0030, mochila inn@hotmail.com, $11 pp dorm, $22 s/d room low season, $32 high season), an English-run hostel with shared kitchen, an upstairs dorm, one private room, and two cabins.

$25-50

The best bet for location in this price range is beachfront **Hotel Moctezuma** (tel./fax 506/2642-0058, $15 s or $20 d with fan, $30 s or $35 d with a/c and TV low season; $20 s or $30 d with fan, $30 s or $45 d with a/c and TV high season), with 28 spacious and clean rooms with fans. The main unit has a restaurant and bar directly over the beach.

The German/Tica–run **Cabinas El Pargo Feliz** (tel. 506/2642-0064, $25–30 s/d low season, $30–35 s/d high season) has eight spacious, clean, basically furnished modern *cabinas* with wooden floors, chipboard walls, fans, queen-size beds, tiled bathroom with cold water only, and hammocks on wide verandas. It has a rustic thatched restaurant.

Hotel L'Aurora (tel./fax 506/2642-0051, www.playamontezuma.net/aurora.htm, $22–50 s/d depending on room size), also run by a German-Tico couple, is a whitewashed house surrounded by lush gardens. It's recently been spruced up. The 18 rooms now have fans and air-conditioning, cable TV, and private baths with hot water. Upstairs is an airy lounge with bamboo and leather sofas, a small library, and hammocks. Rooms downstairs are dark.

$50-100

Hotel Playa Las Manchas (tel. 506/2642-0415, www.beach-hotel-manchas.com, $13 s, $25–50 d low season; $20 s, $40–75 d high season), nearby, has three lovely and distinct cabins in lush gardens. Los Colibris and Las Mariposa are two-bedroom bungalows; Casa Los Unicornos is a two-story house. They're simply furnished rooms and have large windows, a kitchen, and private bath and hot water. There's a disco.

I love the German-run **Hotel Horizontes de Montezuma** (tel. 506/2642-0534, www .horizontes-montezuma.com, $35 s, $45–55 d low season; $45 s, $55–65 d high season), midway between Cóbano and Montezuma. This Victorian-style home has seven rooms around a skylit atrium—saturating the hallway of black-and-white tile with magnesium light—and opening to a wraparound veranda with hammocks. The appealing rooms have whitewashed wooden ceilings with fans, terra-cotta floors, sky-blue fabrics, and bathrooms done up in dark-blue tiles. Nice! A shady restaurant opens to the small pool. A solid bargain!

I like **Casacolores** (tel. 506/2642-0283, www.casacolores.com, $40–60 low season, $50–80 high season) for its four one-bedroom and one two-bedroom wooden cabins on stilts; each is painted a bright tropical color and has a kitchen. It has a swimming pool.

The **El Sano Banano Hotel** (tel. 506/2642-0636, www.ylangylangresort.com, $65 s/d low season, $75 s/d high season), above the restaurant in town, is a bed-and-breakfast with 11 air-conditioned rooms decorated in New Mexican style. They have satellite TV and hot-water showers.

With its landscaped pool and deck in lovely grounds, **Hotel El Jardín** (tel./fax 506/2642-0074, www.hoteleljardin.com, $65–75 s/d low season, $85–95 high season) is the best choice in the village itself. It offers 15 elegant hillside rooms with fans, hammocks on the veranda, refrigerators, and private baths (some with hot water). Each is individually styled in hardwoods and shaded by trees in landscaped grounds with pool and whirlpool tub. It also has two villas.

The relaxing **Hotel Amor de Mar** (tel./ fax 506/2642-0262, www.amordemar.com, $40–80 low season, $45–90 high season), 600 meters west of the village, enjoys a fabulous location on a sheltered headland, with a private tidepool and views along the coast in both directions. The hotel is set in pleasant landscaped lawns, with hammocks beneath shady palms. It has 11 rooms (all but two have private baths, some with hot water), each unique in size and decor and made entirely of hardwoods.

The **Luz de Mono Hotel** (tel. 506/2642-0090, www.luzdemono.com, $75 s/d standard, $140 casita low season; $100 standard, $175 casita high season) has improved and is now one of the better options in town, although readers complain of poor service. Centered on a lofty circular atrium with restaurant with conical roof and bamboo furnishings, it has 12 hotel rooms, plus eight stone *casitas* (some with whirlpool tubs). The Blue Congo Bar hosts stage shows and is the liveliest place around—noise can be a problem if you're trying to sleep. Rates include breakfast and tax.

$100-150

Out of town, I like **Nature Lodge Finca los Caballos** (tel./fax 506/2642-0124, www.naturelodge.net, $70–120 s/d low season, $86–138 high season, including taxes), on a 16-hectare ranch midway between Cóbano and Montezuma. Rooms here feature beautiful coral-stone floors and river-stone showers with poured-concrete sinks, tasteful contemporary furnishings that include Indian spreads on hardwood beds, and delightful patios with hammocks and rockers. Four new rooms have rattan or bamboo king-size beds and travertine balconies. A fan-shaped horizon swimming pool is inset in a multilevel wooden deck with poured-concrete, soft-cushioned sofas and lounge chairs for enjoying the fabulous forest and ocean views. There are trails and fantastic birding, as well as a stable. Meals include a full breakfast. A small spa has been added.

OVER $150

The nicest place is **【 Ylang Ylang Beach Resort** (tel. 506/2642-0636, www.ylangylangresort.com, $140 s/d tents, $190 rooms, $195 suites, $240–270 bungalows low season; $160 s/d tents, $195 rooms, $215 suites, $265–295 bungalows high season), a 10-minute walk along the beach 800 meters east of the village. Owners Lenny and Patricia Iacono have created a totally delightful property spread across eight hectares of beachfront that is a lush fantasia of ginger, pandanus, and riotous greens. It has three three-story suites (for up to four people) with kitchens; a three-bedroom apartment; and eight concrete and river-stone bungalows, all accessed by well-manicured paths lit at night. All have fans, private bath, fridge, coffeemaker, and Guatemalan bedspreads. French doors open to verandas within spitting distance of the ocean. The dome bungalows have private outdoor showers. And deluxe safari tents on decks have been added. The coup de grace is an exquisite freeform pool in a faux-natural setting of rocks with water cascading and foliage tumbling all around. Check in is at El Sano Banano café.

Food

For breakfast, head to the **Bakery Café** (tel. 506/2642-0458, 6 A.M.–6 P.M. Mon.–Sat.) for *gallo pinto*, banana bread, soy burgers, and tuna sandwiches served on a pleasant raised patio; or to **【 El Sano Banano** (tel. 506/2642-0638, 7 A.M.–10 P.M. daily), where I recommend the scrambled tofu breakfast. This popular natural-food restaurant serves garlic bread, pasta, yogurt, veggie curry, and nightly dinner specials. It also has fresh-fruit thirst quenchers and ice cream and prepares lunches to go.

Tiny **Café Iguana** (6 A.M.–9:30 P.M. daily) is a great place to watch the street action in town. It serves waffles and muffins, sandwiches, scrumptious coconut cookies, cappuccinos, espressos, and natural juices.

Vegans will thrill to **Orgánico** (tel. 506/ 2642-1322, 8 A.M.–4 P.M. daily low season, 8 A.M.–6 P.M. daily high season), a bakery serving all-organic dishes, from a sushi bowl with tofu ($9) or stir fry rice and vegetables ($8) to brownies and ice cream. It has a pleasant, airy patio.

Ocelots are only one of many animals found at Cabo Blanco.

For ocean views, head to **Restaurante Moctezuma** (tel. 506/2642-0058, 7:30 A.M.–11 P.M. daily, $3–10), at Hotel Moctezuma; this atmospheric open-air eatery serves local fare and seafood, as does **Restaurant El Parque** (no tel., 7 A.M.–10 P.M. daily), on the village beach.

The best dining around is at **Ylang Ylang** (tel. 506/2642-0068, 7 A.M.–9:30 P.M. daily, $5–15), serving delicious fusion fare in romantic surrounds by the beach. The menu includes chilled gazpacho, fresh sushi, and Asian-inspired jumbo shrimp in pineapple and coconut sauce.

You can buy fresh produce at the organic fruit and vegetable market, held in the park every Saturday at 10 A.M.

Information and Services

Montezuma Sun Trails (tel. 506/2642-0808, 8 A.M.–8 P.M. daily), in the village center, has Internet service, but bring a sweater!

Librería Topsy (tel. 506/2642-0576, 8 A.M.–1 P.M. Mon.–Fri., 8 A.M.–noon Sat.–Sun.) has heaps of used books, plus an amazingly large selection of international newspapers and magazines, from the *New York Times* to *The Economist*.

Getting There and Away

Buses (tel. 506/2642-0740) depart from Avenida 3, Calles 16/18 in San José at 7:30 A.M. and 2:30 P.M. daily; minibuses meet the bus in Cóbano. Return buses depart Montezuma at 6:15 A.M. and 3:30 P.M. Monday–Saturday (buses from Cóbano depart for San José 30 minutes later).

A bus for Cóbano and Montezuma ($4) meets the Paquera ferry, The bus for Paquera departs Montezuma at 5:30 A.M., 8:05 A.M., 10 A.M., noon, 2:15 P.M., and 4 P.M. and departs from Cóbano (from outside the Hotel Caoba) 15 minutes later.

Interbus (tel. 506/2283-5573, www.interbusonline.com) operates minibus shuttles from San José ($45), as does Montezuma Expeditions' **Tur Bus Shuttle.**

Most of the recreational tour companies offer water-taxis. For example, **Chico's Tour** (tel. 506/2642-0556) has a water-taxi to Jacó ($35 pp).

© CHRISTOPHER P. BAKER

sign in Cabo Blanco Absolute Wildlife Reserve

A taxi to Montezuma from Tambor airport costs about $25.

◖ CABO BLANCO ABSOLUTE WILDLIFE RESERVE

This jewel of nature at the very tip of the Nicoya Peninsula is where Costa Rica's quest to bank its natural resources for the future began. The 1,250-hectare Reserva Natural Absoluta Cabo Blanco (8 A.M.–4 P.M. Wed.– Sun., $10 admission)—the oldest protected area in the country—was created in October 1963 thanks to the tireless efforts of Nils Olof Wessberg, a Swedish immigrant commonly referred to as the father of Costa Rica's national park system (see David Rains Wallace's excellent book *The Quetzal and the Macaw: The Story of Costa Rica's National Parks*). Olof Wessberg was murdered in the Osa Peninsula in the summer of 1975 while campaigning to have that region declared a national park. A plaque near the Cabo Blanco ranger station stands in his honor.

The reserve, which includes 1,800 hectares out to sea, is named Cabo Blanco (White Cape) after the vertical-walled island at its tip, which owes its name to the accumulation of guano deposited by seabirds, including Costa Rica's largest community of brown boobies (some 500 breeding pairs). Two-thirds of the reserve is off-limits to visitors. One-third is accessible along hiking trails, some steep in parts. **Sendero Sueco** leads to the totally unspoiled white-sand beaches of Playa Balsita and Playa Cabo Blanco, which are separated by a headland (you can walk around it at low tide). A coastal trail, **Sendero El Barco,** leads west from Playa Balsita to the western boundary of the park. Check tide tables with the park rangers before setting off—otherwise you could get stuck. Torrential downpours are common April–December.

Isla Cabuya, about 200 meters offshore, has been used as a cemetery for the village of Cabuya. You can walk out to the island at low tide.

The gateway to the reserve is **Cabuya,** a tiny hamlet nine kilometers west of Montezuma. A rough rock-and-dirt track leads north over the mountains to Malpaís (seven kilometers; 4WD essential—and passable only in dry season). **Rainsong Wildlife Sanctuary** (tel. 506/2642-1265, www.rainsongsanctuary .com, 8–11 A.M. and 2–5 P.M. daily, $5 donation), one kilometer north of Cabuya, is a rescue center for animals such as monkeys, porcupines, raccoons, and kinkajous. They can be viewed in cages, and you can pet many of them; most were confiscated from illegal ownership or were injured and rescued in the wild. Its primary focus is education, as well as rehabilitation of animals on a 31-acre rainforest plot linked to Cabo Blanco. Volunteers are needed.

Information

The ranger station (tel./fax 506/2642-0093, cablanco@ns.minae.go.cr) has self-guided trail maps. Camping is not allowed, even at the ranger station.

Accommodations and Food

At Cabuya, **Jungalows El Ancla de Oro** (tel. 506/2642-0369, www.caboblancopark.com/ ancla.htm, $25 s/d rooms, $35–50 s/d bungalows low season; $27 s/d rooms, $40–55 bungalows high season) has camping for $5 per tent low season, $8 high season. It also has three delightful thatched hardwood A-frame cabins on tall stilts (one sleeps five). The restaurant serves tasty treats such as fish curry with coconut milk, shrimp curry, and garlic herb bread. The owners, Alex Villaloboso and his English wife, Fiona, rent horses ($20), mountain bikes ($10), and kayaks.

Getting There

A bus departs Montezuma for Cabuya and Cabo Blanco at 8:15 A.M., 10:15 A.M., 2:15 P.M., and 6:15 P.M. ($1 each way). The Cabuya–Montezuma bus departs at 7 A.M., 9 A.M., and 1 P.M.

Montezuma Travel Adventures (tel. 506/642-0802, www.montezumatravel adventures.com) offers transfers by reservation ($6 round-trip). Collective taxis depart Montezuma for Cabo at 7 and 9 A.M., returning at 3 and 4 P.M. ($1.50 pp). A private taxi costs about $12 one-way.

◖ SANTA TERESA AND MALPAÍS

The shoreline immediately north of Cabo Blanco is a lively surfers' paradise with some of the most splendid surfing beaches in the country. The past few years have seen a phenomenal tourist development, propelling Santa Teresa from offbeat obscurity to newfound popularity. Dozens of hotels and restaurants have popped up out of nowhere. Land prices have since skyrocketed, fueled in part by the fact that Mel Gibson, Drew Barrymore, and supermodel Giselle Bündchen are among the recent celebs to buy property here.

A road that leads west 10 kilometers from Cóbano hits the shore at the hamlet of **Carmen,** known in the surfing realm as Malpaís. The tiny fishing hamlet of Malpaís is actually three kilometers south of Carmen, but no matter; this dirt road dead-ends at the hamlet and turns inland briefly, ending at the northern entrance gate to Cabo Blanco Absolute Wildlife Reserve (there is no ranger station, hence no entrance fee). A rocky track that begins 800 meters north of the dead-end links Cabuya with Malpaís. Four-wheel drive is essential.

North from Carmen, the dirt road parallels **Playa Carmen** and **Playa Santa Teresa,** a seemingly endless beach with coral-colored sand, pumping surf, and dramatic rocky islets offshore. The community of Santa Teresa straggles along the road for several miles. The road continues to Manzanillo, where the going gets tougher and is a potholed bouillabaisse in wet season. The Malpaís–Santa Teresa community stretches along miles of shorefront, and local transport is minimal. Be prepared to walk if you don't have wheels.

Entertainment and Events

Malpaís Surf Camp has a lively bar that shows surf videos and has ping-pong, table soccer, a pool table, and (occasionally) a mechanical bull.

La Lora (tel. 506/2640-0132) is the in-vogue bar in Santa Teresa; it has a pool table and theme nights, including a house dance party

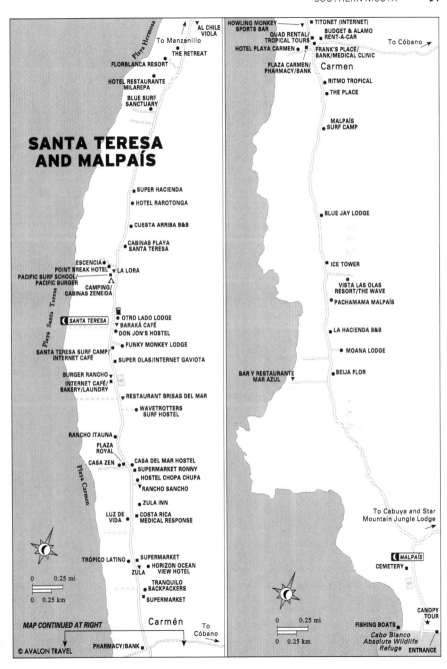

SANTA TERESA AND MALPAÍS

Playa Hermosa

To Manzanillo

AL CHILE VIOLA

THE RETREAT

FLORBLANCA RESORT

HOTEL RESTAURANTE MILAREPA

BLUE SURF SANCTUARY

SUPER HACIENDA

HOTEL RAROTONGA

CUESTA ARRIBA B&B

CABINAS PLAYA SANTA TERESA

ESCENCIA
POINT BREAK HOTEL
PACIFIC SURF SCHOOL/
PACIFIC BURGER
LA LORA
CAMPING/
CABINAS ZENEIDA

Playa Santa Teresa

SANTA TERESA

OTRO LADO LODGE
BARAKÁ CAFÉ
DON JON'S HOSTEL

FUNKY MONKEY LODGE

SANTA TERESA SURF CAMP/
INTERNET CAFÉ

SUPER OLAS/INTERNET GAVIOTA

BURGER RANCHO
INTERNET CAFÉ/
BAKERY/LAUNDRY

RESTAURANT BRISAS DEL MAR

WAVETROTTERS SURF HOSTEL

RANCHO ITAUNA

PLAZA ROYAL

CASA ZEN

CASA DEL MAR HOSTEL
SUPERMARKET RONNY
HOSTEL CHOPA CHUPA
RANCHO SANCHO

ZULA INN

LUZ DE VIDA

COSTA RICA MEDICAL RESPONSE

Playa Carmen

TRÓPICO LATINO

SUPERMARKET

HORIZON OCEAN VIEW HOTEL

ZULA

TRANQUILO BACKPACKERS

SUPERMARKET

0   0.25 mi

0   0.25 km

MAP CONTINUED AT RIGHT

Carmén

To Cóbano

© AVALON TRAVEL

PHARMACY/BANK

HOWLING MONKEY SPORTS BAR

TITONET (INTERNET)

QUAD RENTAL/
TROPICAL TOURS

BUDGET & ALAMO RENT-A-CAR

HOTEL PLAYA CARMEN

To Cóbano

FRANK'S PLACE/
BANK/MEDICAL CLINIC

PLAZA CARMEN/
PHARMACY/BANK

Carmen

RITMO TROPICAL

THE PLACE

MALPAÍS SURF CAMP

BLUE JAY LODGE

ICE TOWER

VISTA LAS OLAS RESORT/THE WAVE

PACHAMAMA MALPAÍS

LA HACIENDA B&B

MOANA LODGE

BAR Y RESTAURANTE MAR AZUL

BEIJA FLOR

To Cabuya and Star Mountain Jungle Lodge

MALPAÍS

CEMETERY

0   0.25 mi

0   0.25 km

CANOPY TOUR

FISHING BOATS

Cabo Blanco Absolute Wildlife Refuge

ENTRANCE

Tuesday; reggae and hip hop on Thursday; and Latin night on Saturday.

Howlin Monkey Sports Bar & Grill (tel. 506/2640-0007) has sporting events on the big screen.

The most upscale and happening place at last visit was **D&N Day & Night Beach Club** (tel. 506/2640-0353, 9 A.M.–2:30 A.M. daily), with live DJs.

Sports and Recreation

Canopy del Pacífico (tel. 506/2640-0360, www.canopydelpacifico.com) offers tours by zipline between the treetops at 9 A.M. and 2 P.M. by reservation ($49).

There are a dozen or more surf shops, several offering tours, including **Adrenalina Surf & Kite School** (tel. 506/8324-8671, laurent_trinci@hotmail.com). **Malpaís Surf Camp** (tel. 506/2642-0031, www.malpaissurfcamp.com) and **Santa Teresa Surf Camp** (tel. 506/2640-0049, surf@expreso.co.cr) also rent boards and offer surf lessons. **Malpaís Quad Tours** (tel. 506/2640-0178) and **Santa Teresa Sunset** (tel. 506/2640-0315, www.santateresasunset.com) rent ATVs and offers tours.

Malpaís Bike Tours (tel. 506/2640-0550, info@malpaisbiketours.com) has bicycling tours.

After all your activities, relax with a massage at **Sonja Spa** (tel. 506/2640-1060, jenifer106@hotmail.com), in Plaza Carmen.

Accommodations

There are many more options than can be listed here.

CAMPING

In Santa Teresa, **Camping y Cabinas Zeneida** (tel. 506/2640-0118) is tucked amid shade trees (with hammocks) beside the beach. It charges $3 pp for camping, including toilets and showers. It also has two A-frame cabins with loft bedrooms and toilets and kitchenettes, plus a thatched cabin ($5 pp). The owners will cook meals.

You can also camp at **Tranquilo Backpackers** (tel. 506/2640-0589, www.tranquilobackpackers.com, $7 pp), and at **Malpaís Surf Camp and Resort** (tel. 506/2642-0031, www.malpaissurfcamp.com, $7 pp). Both have showers and toilets.

UNDER $25

An in spot with budgeting backpackers is **Tranquilo Backpackers** (tel. 506/2640-0589, www.tranquilobackpackers.com, $11 pp dorms, $13 pp loft, $35 s/d private). Rooms are in a two-story New Mexican–style building with dangerously open rails on the balcony—take care up there! It has seven dorms with lofts and bunks, plus clean, airy, spacious private rooms with bathrooms. There's an open-air lounge with hammocks, plus a kitchen, Internet café, and parking.

The well-run **Malpaís Surf Camp and Resort** (tel. 506/2642-0031, www.malpaissurfcamp.com, $15 pp camp beds, $35 s/d cabins with shared bath, $95 d casita), 200 meters south of the junction, has a panoply of accommodations set in eight hectares of grounds. An oceanview *rancho* has "semi-private" camp beds beneath a tin roof with shared baths. There are also *cabinas* with shared bath with cold water, and poolside *casitas* with stone floors, tall louvered screened windows, and beautiful tile bathrooms with hot water. There's a lively bar, a pool, and horse and surfboard rentals.

My fave backpackers' hostel, though, is ◖ **Wavetrotters Surf Hostel** (tel. 506/2640-0805, www.wavetrotterhostel.com, $12 pp), new in 2007. This Italian-run winner is basically an atrium lodge with an open downstairs lounge with soaring ceiling and four all-wooden upstairs dorms with lockers. They open to a common terrace, and you can descend to the lounge via a firepole! Plus there's a private room downstairs ($30 s/d low season, $35 s/d high season). It rents surfboards.

For a great bargain, choose **Casa Zen** (tel. 506/2640-0523, www.zencostarica.com, $12 pp dorm, $24 s/d room, $135 apartment), with an Indian motif, colorful cushions, chessboards, free movies by night, a great Thai restaurant, and four simply furnished sponge-washed rooms (including two dorms) with batiks, ceiling fans, and shared bathrooms. Casa Zen also has an upstairs three-room apartment with a huge terrace with hammocks. It recently added a spa.

$25-50

Once a backpackers' place, **Frank's Place** (tel./fax 506/2640-0096, www.franksplacecr.com, $28 s/d shared bathroom, $30–95 private bathroom), at the junction for Cóbano, has grown beyond recognition and now offers 33 rooms and bungalows in various styles. Alas, the upper-end rooms are overpriced.

I like **Ritmo Tropical** (tel. 506/2640-0174, www.nicoyapeninsula.com/malpais/ritmo tropical, $40 s/d low season, $50 high season), 400 meters south of Frank's Place, with seven modern, cross-ventilated, well-lit cabins in a landscaped complex, each for four people and each with fans, modest furnishings, and nice private bathroom with hot water. It has secure parking, plus an Italian restaurant (Thurs.–Tues.).

Ingo offers eight rooms at **Cabinas Playa Santa Teresa** (tel./fax 2640-0137, $20 s/d, $25 with kitchen low season; $30 s/d, $35 kitchen high season), built around a massive strangler fig favored by howler monkeys. Three have kitchens; all have two double beds and private baths with cold water. It has hammocks under shade, plus parking.

The well-maintained, U.S.–run **Santa Teresa Surf Camp** (tel. 506/2640-0049, surf@expreso.co.cr, $8 hammock, $12 pp shared bath, $48 s/d cabin low season; $10 hammock, $15 pp shared bath, $67 s/d cabin high season) offers wonderful *cabinas* with beautiful color schemes. It has one spacious cabin with sloping tin roof, ceiling fans, cement tile floors, and kitchenette with large fridge; large louvered windows open to a terrace. Four other cabins have clean, shared outside bathrooms with cold-water showers. It also has a beachfront, two-bedroom, air-conditioned house with cable TV, colorful walk-in showers, large kitchen, and wraparound veranda.

$50-100

The lovely **Rancho Itauna** (tel./fax 506/2640-0095, www.ranchos-itauna.com, $70 without kitchen, $80 with kitchen low season; $80 without kitchen, $90 with kitchen high season), in Santa Teresa, is run by a charming Austrian-Brazilian couple and offers four rooms in two octagonal two-story buildings. Each room has a fan, refrigerator, double bed plus bunk, and private bathroom with hot water. Two rooms have a kitchen. The pleasing restaurant serves international cuisine. Rates include tax.

The **Star Mountain Jungle Lodge** (tel. 506/2640-0101, www.starmountaineco.com, $50 s, $65 d), two kilometers northeast of Malpaís, on the track to Cabuya, is a gem tucked in the hills amid an 80-hectare private forest reserve, with trails (the turnoff is 400 meters north of the soccer field in Malpaís). The four charming, cross-ventilated *cabinas* are simply yet tastefully decorated and have Sarchí rockers on the veranda. A *casita* bunkhouse sleeps up to nine people. There's a pool, and guided horseback rides are offered. Grilled meats and fish are prepared in a huge open oven. It offers horseback rides ($30 two hours).

Also a delight, **The Place** (tel. 506/2640-0001, www.theplacemalpais.com, $60–80 s/d room, $120 s/d bungalow low season; $70–90 s/d room, $140 s/d bungalow low season) is a romantic delight. The high point is a lovely jade-colored pool and adjoining open-air lounge with rattan pieces with leopard-skin prints. Rooms are simply furnished and dark but have earth tones, yellows, and graceful batiks. Far nicer are the bungalows, with trendy cement floors, all-around floor-to-ceiling louvered French doors, and pink spreads enlivening whitewashed wooden walls. Each bungalow has its own style—I like the African villa.

Another winner is **Luz de Vida** (tel. 506/2640-0568, www.luzdevida-resort.com, $65 s/d room, $80 s/d bungalow low season; $80 s/d room, $95 s/d bungalow high season), with delightfully decorated split-level bungalows surrounded by forest, plus a splendid colorful restaurant overlooking a handsome pool, gorgeously floodlit at night.

Worthy alternatives include **Pachamama** (tel. 506/2640-0195, www.pacha-malpais .com); **Funky Monkey Lodge** (tel. 506/2640-0272, www.funky-monkey-lodge.com), with some of the loveliest rooms and dorms around; and **Tropical Surf House** (tel. 506/8345-7746, www.tropicalpasta.com).

$100-150

A tasteful newcomer, the Argentinian-run **Blue Surf Sanctuary** (tel. 506/2640-1001, www .bluesurfsanctuary.com, $110–135 s, $125–150 d) is a delight. It has an open kitchen-lounge with hammocks and sofas, plus four individually themed and raised villas with pendulous open-air queen-size lounge beds slung beneath. Lovely furnishings include dark contemporary hardwoods, ethnic pieces and fabrics, and gorgeous albeit small bathrooms with mosaic tiles and large walk-in showers. It has a plunge pool and surf school.

The delightful **Trópico Látino Lodge** (tel. 506/2640-0062, www.hoteltropicolatino.com, $77–120 s/d low season, $103–155 s/d high season), at Playa Santa Teresa, backs a rocky foreshore with hammocks under shade trees. There's a pool and whirlpool tub, and a breezy bar and restaurant (serving excellent cuisine) by the shore. It has 10 high-ceilinged, simply furnished wooden bungalows amid lawns; each has wide shady verandas, a king-size bed and a sofa bed, mosquito nets, fans, and a private bath with hot water. Two newer cabins have ocean views. It arranges fishing, horseback rides, and tours. Rates include tax.

The best hotel in this price bracket is the gorgeous, African-themed 【 **Moana Lodge** (tel. 506/2640-0230, www.moanalodge.com, $95 s/d standard, $125 deluxe, $165–265 suite low season; $115 s/d standard, $140 deluxe, $195–295 suite high season), with seven rooms, some in huge colonial-style wooden cabins, featuring four-poster beds with cowhide drapes, zebra (fake) skins, leopard-print cushions, free Wi-Fi, and large well-lit bathrooms with huge showers. An open-air rancho with poured concrete sofa overlooks a large whirlpool tub and freeform pool in a stone-faced sundeck. Nice! And a bargain!

A newcomer, the Asian-inspired **Beija Flor** (tel. 506/2640-1007, www.beijaflorresort.com, $85–105 s/d rooms, $120 s/d bungalows, $135 s/d suite, $185 villa) specializes in yoga and wellness retreats. The air-conditioned guest quarters have a stylish contemporary motif of whites and taupes, and most have Wi-Fi.

The **Hotel Playa Carmen** (tel. 506/2640-0404, www.playacarmenhotel.com, $90 s/d room, $125–250 suite low season; $140 s/d room, $195–275 suite high season), at Plaza Carmen, has clean contemporary lines. Although guest rooms are dark, they have ceiling fans and bathrooms with glass walls and travertine, and they open to a lovely courtyard with pool, hot tub, and a circular thatched bar.

Also new in 2008, the Israeli-run **Zula Inn Aparthotel** (tel. 506/2640-0940, www.zula inn.com, $90 s/d low season, $110 high season), at Playa Santa Teresita, is another lovely hotel worth considering.

OVER $150

The French-owned **Hotel Restaurante Milarepa** (tel. 506/2640-0023, www.milarepa hotel.com, $170–200 low season, $194–224 high season), at the north end of Playa Santa Teresa, exemplifies tasteful simplicity and has four cabins, spaced apart amid lawns inset with a lap pool. Two cabins are literally on the beach. They're made of bamboo and rise from a cement base: exquisite albeit sparse appointments invoke a Japanese motif, and there are four-poster beds in the center of the room, with mosquito drapes, plus open-air bathroom-showers in their own patio gardens. One wall folds back entirely to offer ocean vistas. It has a splendid restaurant.

Then there's the **Otro Lado Lodge** (tel. 506/2640-1941, www.otroladolodge.com, $100 s/d low season, $120 s/d high season), another lovely contemporary-style newcomer with a crisp aesthetic, combing gleaming whites with colorful tropical highlights. The restaurant here is a winner.

Yoga fans might check out **Horizon Ocean View Hotel** (tel. 506/2640-0524, www .horizon-yogahotel.com, $80–150 low season,

© CHRISTOPHER P. BAKER

La Reserva

$100–180 high season), a dedicated hilltop yoga center with simply appointed cabins.

"Stunning" and "serene" are fitting descriptions for ❨ **Florblanca Resort** (tel. 506/2640-0232, www.florblanca.com, $475–850 s/d), perhaps the finest boutique beach resort in the country. This gem enjoys an advantageous beachfront position at the north end of Santa Teresa. Imbued with a calming Asiatic influence (Tibetan prayer flags flutter over the entrance), it offers 10 luxury oceanside villas stairstepping down to the beach. Fragrant plumeria and namesake *flor-blanca* trees drop petals at your feet as you walk stone pathways that curl down through an Asian garden. The motif is Santa Fe–meets–Bali in ochers, soft creams, and yellows. The villas are furnished with silent air-conditioning, large wall safes, quality rattan furnishings, tasteful art pieces, and exquisite furnishings, from lamps of tethered bamboo stalks to king-size beds on raised hardwood pedestals. Each has a kitchenette, a vast lounge, and stone-floored "rainforest" bathroom with lush gardens, and separate showers and oversize tub. Resort facilities

include a TV lounge, quality souvenir store, and a walk-in landscaped horizon pool fed by a waterfall with swim-up bar. The superb oceanfront restaurant and sushi bar is worth a visit in its own right. New owner, Rusty Carter, from Carolina, was adding a deluxe spa and a sumptuous bi-level honeymoon suite at last visit. Tours, including horseback riding at the cattle roundup at Hacienda Ario ($60 three hours), plus yoga, kickboxing, and dance classes in a world-class dojo are all available. Pricing here has been fickle, as guests stayed away when Rusty raised the rates a tad too much.

In 2008, Rusty opened ❨ **La Reserva** (tel. 506/2640-0232, www.florblanca.com, call for rates), a super and super-exclusive adjunct (formerly Latitude 10) with three junior suites, two master suites, and a deluxe room (actually, they're all private villas) hidden within its own forest garden. With its pampering personalized service, this is the ultimate in deluxe, private lodgings in Nicoya. Villas are infused with Asian influences, including dark colonial plantation furnishings, glassless windows and French doors, king-size beds a mile off the

nouvelle cuisine at Néctar, Florblanca Resort

© CHRISTOPHER P. BAKER

floor, and fabulous open-air bathrooms with rainforest showers. A highlight is the guest-only restaurant. Imagine coconut-carrot-ginger soup ($10), pan-seared snook with black Thai rice, and butter-poached asparagus and jalapeño beurre blanc ($26).

Care to splash out big money for a private villa? Try **The Red Palm Villas** (tel. 506/2640-0447, www.redpalmvillas.com, $105–185 s/d apartments, $350–675 s/d villas), next to Florblanca, with gorgeous beachfront villas seemingly inspired by Frank Lloyd Wright. I also love **Casa Pura Vida Beachfront Luxury Villas** (tel. 506/2640-0511, www.casaspuravida.com), with three gorgeous villas, "each quite different in style," in Santa Teresa.

Food

Malpaís Surf Camp (7 A.M.–10 P.M. daily) serves American breakfasts (from $5), plus lunch and dinner. And I like **Casa Zen** (tel. 506/2640-0523, 7 A.M.–10 P.M. daily), a marvelous Thai restaurant by night, but serving American-style breakfasts ($4) such as veggie

scramble and pancakes and lunches that include BLTs and tuna sandwiches. For dinner ($8), try the seared yellowfin tuna or red coconut curry.

Jungle Juice (tel. 506/2640-0279) serves health foods like pancakes, veggie burgers, quesadillas, and fresh juices. And for a great option for burgers, veggie dishes, kabobs, and slow-cooked chicken, try **Burger Rancho** (tel. 506/2640-0583, 8 A.M.–midnight daily), a tiny little spot that gets packed, despite the road dust.

The restaurant at **Rancho Itauna** (506/2640-0095, 7:30–9:30 A.M. and 6:30–9 P.M. daily, high season only) specializes in Brazilian seafood dishes but also has a barbecue on Thursday.

The open-air **Restaurante Soma** (tel. 506/2640-0023, 7–10 A.M., 11:30 A.M.–2:30 P.M., and 6–9 P.M. daily) at the Hotel Milarepa specializes in Pacific Rim fusion cuisine. Reservations are recommended.

Despite its simple thatched ambience, **Restaurant Brisas del Mar** (tel. 506/2640-0941, 5–10 P.M. does a mean job of nouvelle fusion dishes, such as lemon rosemary chicken with herbed yogurt ($11.50); seared tuna with red wine, capers, and anchovy ($12.50); and self-described "sinfully wicked desserts."

The best cuisine by far is at **❤ Néctar** (7 A.M.–3 P.M. daily café only, 3–6 P.M. daily sushi only, 6–9 P.M. daily full menu) at Florblanca, where Chef Spencer Graves conjures up fabulous Asian-Pacific-Latin fusion creations, including smoked trout, cream cheese, and scallion maki roll appetizers ($7), and salmon, scallion, and caviar jumbo roll ($9). Entrées include Chinese five-spice marinated duck breast with caramelized red onion latkes and butter-wilted spinach ($20). The raised hemispheric bar is a good place to enjoy top-quality sushi (don't fail to order the caterpillar rolls). A chef's five-course tasting menu is offered with 24 hours' notice. It plays cool music, from jazz to classical.

The past few years have seen an explosion of sushi restaurants that include **Omi Sushi,** in Plaza Carmen; **Sushi Ukiy** (tel. 506/2640-0690, 6–10 P.M. Thurs.–Sun.); and **Cameleon Restaurant & Sushi Bar** (tel. 506/2640-0949, 6–10:30 P.M. Mon.–Sat.).

In Plaza Carmen, **Artemis Café** (tel. 506/2640-0561, 7 A.M.–midnight daily) is clean and modern and has Wi-Fi plus an outdoor courtyard. The wide-ranging menu includes paninis, salads, smoked salmon appetizer ($8), and dinners such as spinach ravioli ($7.50), as well as cookies.

Across the way, the **Azucar Restaurant** (tel. 506/2640-0071, www.azucar-restaurant.com, 8 A.M.–9:30 P.M. daily) opened at Frank's Place in 2007; it's run by a French-Cuban couple. Norbis is the Cuban (yet London-trained) chef at the helm delivering delicious nouvelle tropical cuisine, such as seared ahi tuna with ginger ($12), and mahimahi with basil mashed potatoes with tomato and parsley sauce ($10). It's a great spot to try *ropa vieja* or a burger, then a chocolate tart with ice cream before bedding down poolside for a snooze.

You can buy fresh produce at the organic fruit and vegetable market, held in Santa Teresa every Saturday at 3 P.M.

Information and Services

There's a **bank** at Plaza Carmen, where **Carmen Connections** (tel. 506/8823-8600) is a tour information center.

There's a **medical clinic** (tel. 800/367-2000) with ambulance service next to Frank's Place, and a **pharmacy** across the street in Plaza Carmen, which has a bank. **Costa Rica Medical Response** (tel. 506/2665-2626) also has 24/7 ambulance service. Teeth trouble? Head to **Sunny Smile Dental Clinic** (tel. 506/2640-0660), in Plaza Royal.

There are half-a-dozen or so Internet cafés, including **Frank's Internet Café,** at the Carmén junction, and **Cyber-Phone Santa Teresa** (tel. 506/2640-0996).

The **Santa Teresa Surf Camp** doubles as a Spanish-language school.

You can buy gasoline at a *pulpería* 0.5 kilometer north of the soccer field.

Getting There and Away

Buses depart Cóbano for Malpaís at 10:30 A.M. and 2:30 P.M. Return departures are at 7 A.M. and noon, connecting with onward buses to San José.

Montezuma Expeditions (tel. 506/2642-0919, www.montezumaexpeditions.com) has a daily minibus shuttle from San José ($40), as does **Interbus** (tel. 506/2283-5573, www.interbusonline.com, $45).

You can rent an ATV (a virtual necessity in wet season) from **Malpaís Quad Tours** (tel. 506/2640-0178) and **Santa Teresa Sunset** (tel. 506/2640-0315, www.santateresasunset.com). And **Alamo Rent-a-Car** (tel. 506/2640-0526) and **Budget** (tel. 506/2640-0500, www.budget.co.cr) have offices at Carmen.

Taíno Gas (tel. 506/2640-0009), in Santa Teresa, is open 7 A.M.–6 P.M. daily.

www.moon.com

DESTINATIONS | ACTIVITIES | BLOGS | MAPS | BOOKS

MOON.COM is all new, and ready to help plan your next trip! Filled with fresh trip ideas and strategies, author interviews, informative blogs, a detailed map library, and descriptions of all the Moon guidebooks, Moon.com is all you need to get out and explore the world—or even places in your own backyard. As always, when you travel with Moon, expect an experience that is uncommon and truly unique.

MAP SYMBOLS

▦▦▦ Expressway	𝐂 Highlight	✕ Airfield	⚓ Golf Course
▦▦▦ Primary Road	○ City/Town	✕ Airport	🅿 Parking Area
─── Secondary Road	◉ State Capital	▲ Mountain	⬛ Archaeological Site
▪ ▪ ▪ Unpaved Road	⊛ National Capital	✚ Unique Natural Feature	▮ Church
------ Trail	★ Point of Interest		▯ Gas Station
········· Ferry	• Accommodation	⏚ Waterfall	Glacier
~~ Railroad	▼ Restaurant/Bar	⚑ Park	Mangrove
▦▦▦ Pedestrian Walkway	▪ Other Location	ⓣ Trailhead	Reef
))))) Stairs	Λ Campground	⛷ Skiing Area	Swamp

CONVERSION TABLES

°C = (°F - 32) / 1.8
°F = (°C x 1.8) + 32
1 inch = 2.54 centimeters (cm)
1 foot = 0.304 meters (m)
1 yard = 0.914 meters
1 mile = 1.6093 kilometers (km)
1 km = 0.6214 miles
1 fathom = 1.8288 m
1 chain = 20.1168 m
1 furlong = 201.168 m
1 acre = 0.4047 hectares
1 sq km = 100 hectares
1 sq mile = 2.59 square km
1 ounce = 28.35 grams
1 pound = 0.4536 kilograms
1 short ton = 0.90718 metric ton
1 short ton = 2,000 pounds
1 long ton = 1.016 metric tons
1 long ton = 2,240 pounds
1 metric ton = 1,000 kilograms
1 quart = 0.94635 liters
1 US gallon = 3.7854 liters
1 Imperial gallon = 4.5459 liters
1 nautical mile = 1.852 km

°FAHRENHEIT	°CELSIUS	
230	110	
220	100	WATER BOILS
210		
200	90	
190	80	
180		
170	70	
160		
150	60	
140		
130	50	
120		
110	40	
100		
90	30	
80		
70	20	
60		
50	10	
40		
30	0	WATER FREEZES
20		
10	-10	
0		
-10	-20	
-20	-30	
-30		
-40	-40	

INCH
0 1 2 3 4

CM
0 1 2 3 4 5 6 7 8 9 10

MOON COSTA RICA'S NICOYA PENINSULA
Avalon Travel
a member of the Perseus Books Group
1700 Fourth Street
Berkeley, CA 94710, USA
www.moon.com

Editors: Sabrina Young, Michelle Cadden
Series Manager: Kathryn Ettinger
Copy Editor: Valerie Sellers Blanton
Graphics Coordinator: Kathryn Osgood
Production Coordinators: Darren Alessi,
 Amber Pirker
Cover Designer: Kathryn Osgood
Map Editor: Albert Angulo
Cartographers: Chris Markiewicz, Kat Bennett

ISBN: 978-1-59880-328-0

Text © 2009 by Christopher P. Baker.
Maps © 2009 by Avalon Travel.
All rights reserved.

Some photos and illustrations are used by permission and are the property of the original copyright owners.

Front cover photo: © Villa Alegre
Title page: © Christopher P. Baker

Printed in the United States

ABOUT THE AUTHOR

Christopher P. Baker

Since 1983, Christopher P. Baker has made his living as a professional travel writer, photographer, lecturer, and tour guide, and is acclaimed for his specialist knowledge of Cuba and Costa Rica, about which he has written 10 books. He has contributed to more than 150 publications worldwide including *Caribbean Travel & Life, Elle, Maxim, National Geographic Traveler, The Robb Report,* and the *Los Angeles Times.* He has been profiled in *USA Today,* and appears frequently on radio and television talk shows and as a guest lecturer aboard cruise ships. Christopher currently escorts cruise-tours to Costa Rica and Panama on behalf of National Geographic Expeditions, and has been privileged to address such organizations as the National Press Club, the World Affairs Council, and the National Geographic Society's *Live... From National Geographic.*

Christopher was born and raised in Yorkshire, England. He received a BA in geography at University College, London, and master's degrees in Latin American studies from Liverpool University and in education from the Institute of Education, London University. He began his writing career in 1978 as Contributing Editor on Latin America for *Land & Liberty,* a London-based political journal. In 1980 he received a Scripps-Howard Foundation Scholarship in Journalism to attend the University of California, Berkeley.

Christopher is the author of more than 20 books, including *Moon Costa Rica, Moon Cuba* and *Mi Moto Fidel: Motorcycling Through Castro's Cuba,* winner of two national book awards. In 2008, he was named the prestigious Lowell Thomas Travel Journalist of the Year by the Society of American Travel Writers Foundation. His other awards include the 1995 Benjamin Franklin Best Travel Guide Award (for *Moon Costa Rica*) and the Caribbean Tourism Organization's 2005 Travel Journalist of the Year. You can learn more about Christopher's work on his website, www.christopherbaker.com.